Reproductive Health Education

Adolescents' Knowledge, Perception and Programmes

Manju Goel

SHIPRA

Rs. 650; US$ 32.50

ISBN: 978-81-7541-739-7

First Published in India in 2014

Reproductive Health Education:
Adolescents' Knowledge, Perception and Programmes

Published by:
SHIPRA PUBLICATIONS
H.O.: LG 18-19, Pankaj Central Market, Patparganj,
I.P. Ext., Delhi-110092, Tel: 91-11-2223 5152, 2223 6152
Br.Off.: 4617/18, Ansari Road, Darya Ganj,
New Delhi-110002, Tel: 9650028065, 9810522367
E-mail: info@shiprapublications.com
www.shiprapublications.com

Preface

> *"Reproductive health education should flow as river flows, if we try to stop students learning about reproductive health issues, it will not stop so better to give a direction to the flow from the starting point itself."*
> —*Respondent (a teacher)*

Adolescence is a period of growth and development from the onset of puberty to transition into adulthood. During this period adolescents attain reproductive and sexual maturity. It is universally agreed that all adolescents need accurate and adequate information about reproductive and sexual health. In the absence of adequate and accurate information adolescents are at risk of being worry-informed about sexual and reproductive matters, which likely to lead them to make decisions that could have negative effects on their lives. As regards to the adolescents' awareness about their reproductive health issues, it is urged that education is the major viable media for this purpose. There is a need to impart reproductive health education to adolescents. It is realized that it should be imparted by the important stakeholders i.e., parents and teachers. Thus, the book explores the opinion of all the three major stakeholders including adolescents, parents and teachers. It examines the adolescents' reproductive health issues, including the knowledge, perception and context within which they arise and also explores the opinion of parents, teachers, and adolescents on imparting reproductive health education. It also covers the existing policies and programmes with respect to reproductive health education for adolescents.

This volume has been divided into 7 chapters. *Chapter – 1* introduces to the concept of reproductive health education, reproductive health status of adolescents in India, theoretical perspectives, scientific background, rationale of the study, relevance to social work practice, and research methodology. In *Chapter – 2* the author provided an appraisal from the relevant researches which included the articles, books, empirical studies related to reproductive health education for adolescents. *Chapter – 3* presents a brief analysis of the national policies and programmes on reproductive health education for adolescents. *Chapter – 4* presents the profile of the adolescents, parents and teachers. *Chapter – 5* deals with the knowledge and perception of adolescent students on reproductive health issues which include: process of growing up, pregnancy, abortion, contraceptives, sexual behaviour, sexual abuse/ harassment, sexually transmitted infections (STIs), HIV/AIDS, and substance abuse. An attempt has been made in *Chapter – 6* to examine the opinion of parents, teachers, and adolescents towards imparting reproductive health education. *Chapter – 7* outlines the imperative findings, discussion and recommendations including the social work intervention model.

Dr. Manju Goel

Acknowledgements

I would like to pen down a few words of profound gratitude to The Almighty for enabling me to complete the book.

I deem it is a great pleasure to acknowledge my deep gratitude to Prof. Sushma Batra, Head, Department of Social Work, University of Delhi, for her keen guidance and valuable suggestions at every stage of the study. Her uninterrupted encouragement towards perfection and her personal warmth have been a source of motivation to me throughout the course of this investigation.

I owe my gratitude to Dr. Manoj K. Jha, Professor, Department of Social Work, University of Delhi for facilitating the translation of the tools of data collection in Hindi and encouragement to complete the research successfully.

I would like to acknowledge my thanks to a number of experts who have enriched this work with their comments and suggestions. These include: Dr. (Mrs.) Pawan Sudhir, Project Coordinator, School Adolescence Education Programme, SCERT for her valuable support in providing Yuva modules and expert opinion on the research topic, Dr. Pankaj Arora, Associate Professor, CIE, University of Delhi, for his insightful ideas at the initial phase, Mr. Bilal Ahmed, NACO for sharing his experience of working on the issue of Adolescence Education Programme, Dr. Sushma Yadav, Project Director, Adolescence Education Program, NCERT, for sharing her experiences of adolescence education programme and discussing about preparing appropriate tools of data collection.

I appreciate the constant encouragement by Mr. D. Kumar, the publisher of this book.

My deepest appreciation is all for my family members for always being a constant source of support and encouragement. My special thanks and appreciation are due to my husband Naveen Goel, who had nurtured this work in all possible ways to ensure its fruitful outcome. I attribute all my success to him. My son Kinshuk deserves a special mention for always pepping me up with his cute smile and melodious laughter.

Last but not least I am thankful to all those who remained unnamed for their co-operation and generous help.

Dr. Manju Goel

Contents

1

Introduction

"Reproductive health is a state of complete physical, mental and social well being and not merely the absence of disease or infirmity, in all matters relating to the reproductive system and to its functions and processes... It also improves sexual health, the purpose of which is the enhancement of life and personal relation, and not merely counseling and care related to reproductive and sexually transmitted diseases" (WHO, 1996).

The above definition of reproductive health contained in the programme of the International Conference on Population and Development (ICPD), Cairo is an improved version of the World Health Organization's technical definition, which was accepted by the United Nations general assembly. It is being followed by government and voluntary agencies world over and also utilized as a functional definition for the study.

The reproductive health thus includes a much wider area than only physical well-being. Reproductive health addresses the physical, social, emotional and psychological dimensions of sex and reproduction and not just the presence or absence of disease of reproductive organs. The proponents of the reproductive health framework believe that reproductive health is inextricably linked to the subject of reproductive rights and freedom. Also, the reproductive health concept extends beyond the narrow confines of family planning to encompass all aspects of human sexuality and reproductive health needs during the various stages of the life cycle. ICPD Programme declares that all countries "should protect and promote the rights of adolescents to reproductive health education, information and care and greatly reduce the number of adolescent pregnancies".

Reproductive health education, through schools is the education imparted to adolescents as part of their educational curriculum to promote safer sexual behaviours among adolescents. Reproductive health education is a key strategy for promoting safe sexual behaviour among adolescents. It is an attempt to respect and care about one's basic needs contributing to healthy body and mind. School-based instruction is a primary mode of reproductive health education. Reproductive health education is the front line of efforts to prevent pregnancy, AIDS and other sexually transmitted infections (STIs) among adolescents, including messages to encourage abstinence and promote the use of condoms and contraceptives by those who are sexually active. Reproductive health education becomes most crucial now, due to rapid demographic changes, media, and globalization. It is an individual's decision to reproduce or share physical expression. With growing individual autonomy and participation of adolescents it becomes a responsibility of the socializing agents to provide a guiding light towards a bright and stable future.

The present concept of reproductive health education saw a scientific and global beginning with population studies and population education. It focused on developing individual's framework towards population and its impact on oneself. As defined by UNESCO seminar (1970), population education is an educational programme which provides for a study of the population situation in a family, community, nation and the world, with the purpose of developing in the students rational and responsible attitude and behaviour towards that situation (Swamy, 2005).

A number of seminars have been conducted and committees formed to introduce population education in school curriculum. Family Planning Association of India (FPAI), Ministry of Health and Family Planning, Ministry of Education and Youth Services, NCERT, and others are some of the prime organisations responsible to articulate and showcase the vision of reproductive health education. Small family norms saw its presence in the national education policy, 1986, for the first time. Since then there has been a significant shift from population dynamics on individual to individual's reproductive health needs embracing physical, psychological, and social aspects.

The reproductive health issues gained recognition in 1980s, momentum in the 1990s and was crystallized at the International Conference on Population and Development (ICPD) 1994. The concept of reproductive health attracted a wide attention during the ICPD conference (1994). ICPD 1994 emphasized on addressing adolescent reproductive health issues by promotion of responsible and healthy reproductive and sexual behaviour. The conference also raised concern for protecting the human rights and well being of adolescents and encouraging the active participation of adolescents in the process of socio-economic development. The rights of adolescents have been focused as the most controversial topic in U.N. Conventions. During ICPD, the following sensitive rights of adolescents were recognized:

- The right to the enjoyment of the highest attainable standard of health,
- The right to the privacy, confidentiality and informed consent,

- The right to reproductive health education, information and care (UN, 1994).

A World Health Assembly resolution of May 1995 presents an outline of the global reproductive health strategy. This Global strategy focuses on three main interrelated areas:

- Advocacy for the concept of, and for political commitment to, reproductive health, for an "enabling" environment, for wide participation and for increased resources for reproductive health programmes,
- Research and action to support promotion and protection of reproductive health, prevention of specific reproductive health problems, and care and rehabilitation for all when needed, and
- Attention to the special reproductive health needs and concerns of women, to underserved groups such as adolescents, to the roles and responsibilities of men, and to such population groups as refugees and displaced people.

In National Curriculum Framework for School Education, N.C.E.R.T. (2000) on Population Education

- Chapter 1.4.10. under the caption ' Integrated Diverse Curriculum Concerns,' it states, "At a time when concerns such as 'literacy' 'family system', 'neighborhood education', 'environment education', 'human rights education', 'legal literacy', 'peace education', 'migration education', 'global education' and 'safety education' are making a case for separate place in the school curriculum, the best approach would be to integrate these ideas and concepts, after a careful analysis in the existing areas of learning. Appropriate strategies for this integration may be suitably worked out in the detailed subject curricula."
- Chapter 2.5. Under the caption 'general objectives of education, it includes (a) appreciation of the various consequences of large families and over-population and need for checking population growth. (b) Cultivating the power of understanding of and attitude towards healthy sex related issues and respectful attitude toward members of the opposite sex (NCERT, 2000).

Owing to the controversies on adolescent sexuality, the reproductive and sexual health needs of adolescents, very few countries in the World have set up adequate reproductive health care services for adolescents (Pati, 2004). Adolescent reproductive health care needs vary with culture, age, marital status. But it is universally agreed that all adolescents need accurate and adequate information about reproductive and sexual health. In the absence of adequate and accurate information adolescents are at risk of being worry-informed about sexual and reproductive matters, which may lead them to make decisions that could have negative effects on their lives. As regards the adolescents' awareness about their reproductive health issues, it is urged that education is the major viable media for this purpose.

Reproductive Health Status of Adolescents in India

The World Health Organization defines adolescence as the period of life between ages 10 and 19. Adolescence is a stage of development transition i.e. a bridge between childhood and adulthood. It is a progress from appearance of secondary sex characteristics (Puberty) to sexual and reproductive maturity. It is the stage of development of adult mental process and adult identity and transition from total socio-economic dependence to relative independence (WHO, 1986 and, Gupta *et al.,* 2004). Adolescence has traditionally been regarded as a period of stress and strain, a time of heightened emotional tension. As termed by Erikson (1968), the identity crisis or the problem of "Ego-Identity" is a psychological moratorium, a gap between security of childhood and the autonomy of adulthood. Adolescence is a phase when rights of the childhood start shaping while responsibilities and rights of the adults are yet to become accessible. One is 'old enough' for certain things and 'still too small' for certain other things. This phase continues through the second decade of every individual's life. This age group is particularly vulnerable to conditions in their social and physical environments, due to exposure to wide range of positive and negative determinants of health. The interaction of these determinants at each developmental stage helps to define both their level of health and its impact on the later life. The key determinants including social status, income, employment, environment at work, education, social set up, natural and built up environment, personal health practices, individual capacity and coping skills, biological and genetic endowments (Acharya and Dasgupta, 2005). Although adolescents are 1/5th of world's population still it is pertinent to note that many girls are grossly underweight at adolescence (Jejeebhoy, 1995).

Adolescents are an important resource of any country. They have successfully passed the adversaries of childhood and are on their way to adulthood. This is the stage when physical changes are taking place in their development. On this way they may face troubles due to lack of right kind of information regarding their own physical and or sexual development. Going through physical and sexual development, many adolescents become sexually active increasingly at early ages. Their vulnerability, and ignorance on matters related to their reproductive health, their inadequate knowledge on contraception, and inability or unwillingness to use family planning and health services leads adolescents to face reproductive morbidity and mortality (Onifade, 1999). Jejeebhoy (1996) in his study showed that adolescent fertility in India occurs mainly within the context of marriage and over half of all women aged 15-19 years have experienced pregnancy or birth of a child. Unfortunately, their education lacks inputs on reproductive health this is despite their strong desires to participate in activities geared towards their own reproductive health and social development needs. It is feared that adolescent girls as well as boys if not duly informed find themselves at risk of pregnancy, child bearing and getting infected by sexually transmitted diseases.

From the above discussion it is clear that adolescents are still growing up without the opportunities, information, skills, health services and support they need to go through sexual development and postpone sex until they are physically and socially mature and able to make well informed, responsible decisions. Moreover many traditional practices and myths surround normal physiological process such as menarche and when adolescent are not given scientific explanation of such phenomenon, they are left puzzled and are unable to differentiate between myth and reality. This has resulted in anxiety and psychological trauma in adults, who as teenagers had held firmly to certain belief about sexuality (Basanayake, 1985). Due to aforesaid reasons, it is felt that there is a need for creating a generation with proper knowledge for good health.

Thus, initiatives on reproductive health education are an unavoidable call to address the physical and psychological questions arising in adolescents restoring their equilibrium. It is an effort to break through the closed and narrow channels of information coming out of a rigid social framework. The taboo on understanding reproductive needs and patterns often results in curious rebels disrupting one's health and growth. Providing reproductive health education would give a logical and responsible shift to mass media which is often misleading or inadequate, promoting risky behaviour. Considering the multifaceted impact of reproductive health and its varied sources of information, including it in main stream education is an urgent need of the hour. Hence, from the forgoing discussion it is clear that reproductive health is an emerging issue among adolescent.

After having mentioned the meaning, intent, and importance of reproductive health, it is often assumed the reproductive health is the effect of an adult's decisions. But there is need to focus on adolescents as they are future adults. It is important that adolescents should be allowed to study reproductive health. It, therefore, becomes important to first understand the adolescence before introducing the details of the study.

Theoretical Perspectives

The theoretical perspectives on adolescents and adolescence enlighten that adolescence is often described, as an exciting transitory phase in the human life cycle but is perhaps one of the most challenging stage. This is a time when adolescents evolve into adults with newly discovered independence and renewed responsibilities. They are constantly in search of their own new identity. They tend to question and appreciate the values of the adult world and try to assert their existence. During adolescence they develop skills that will help them to grow into caring and responsible adults. When adolescents are supported and encouraged by caring adults, they thrive in unmanageable ways, becoming resourceful and contributing as members of their families and societies.

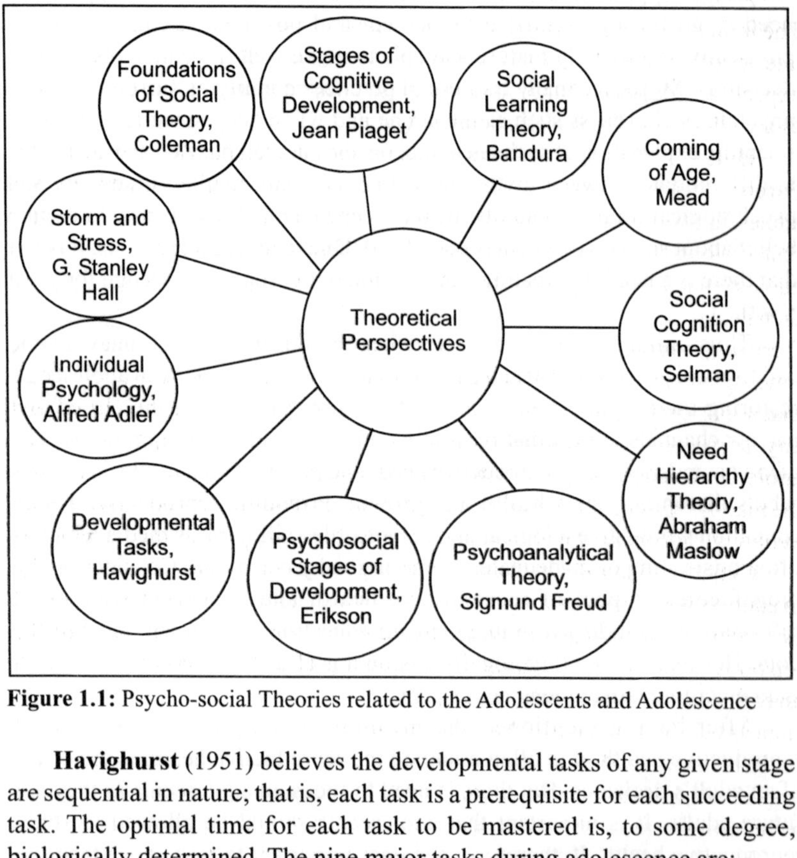

Figure 1.1: Psycho-social Theories related to the Adolescents and Adolescence

Havighurst (1951) believes the developmental tasks of any given stage are sequential in nature; that is, each task is a prerequisite for each succeeding task. The optimal time for each task to be mastered is, to some degree, biologically determined. The nine major tasks during adolescence are:

- Accepting one's physical makeup and acquiring a masculine or feminine sex role.
- Developing appropriate relations with age-mates of both sexes.
- Becoming emotionally independent of parents and other adults.
- Achieving the assurance that one will become economically independent.
- Determining and preparing for a career and entering the job market.
- Developing the cognitive skills and concepts necessary for social competence.
- Understanding and achieving socially responsible behaviour.
- Preparing for marriage and family.
- Acquiring values that are harmonious with an appropriate scientific world picture.

At any given time, adolescents may be dealing with several of these tasks. The importance of specific developmental tasks varies with early, middle and late periods of the transition (Ingersoll, n.d.). The Developmental Tasks Model expects an adolescent who mastered these tasks to emerge from adolescence as a well-adjusted and well-socialized adult.

Hall (1904) saw adolescence as a period of "storm and stress" (S&S). Parents, peers, teachers and society exert considerable pressure on the adolescent to grow up during adolescence. However, **Coleman** (1978) clarified that various stresses in adolescence do not occur at the same time. Rather, adolescents deal with one or two stressful events, which alleviate the stress, then deal with the others. The peak age for stressful situations varies. Although there may be some overlaps, it is unlikely that several would peak at the same time and very rarely do they concentrate at one time. Coleman's view implies that adolescence is not a relatively short period of time and adolescence is not any more or less stressful than any other developmental stage. Some adolescents may have very difficult and stressful experience, but in general, the majority do not. Hence, adolescence seems to represent a series of smoothly evolving changes in development.

Gender differences in the rate of biological growth may spell differences in adult expectations for acceptable behaviour of adolescent females and males. For example, young girls often are expected to behave more like adults than are boys of the same age. Similarly, the timing of maturation, whether one is an early or late maturer, influences social interaction with parents, other adults such as teachers, and peers. Early physical maturers are often treated as more socially and emotionally mature than they are, or than their age mates. This may result in unreasonable expectations being imposed on them, which may have lasting effects on their personality.

Freud (1948) believed that often an important stressor during adolescence is the increase in sexuality. Freud noted that this brings about a recurrence of the oedipal situation, which must be resolved through attraction to opposite sex peers. The increase in the sex drive creates stress and anxiety (fear of opposite sex and fear of feeling sexual), which may call into play one or more defense mechanisms to restore equilibrium and protect the individual from experiencing anxiety. Use of defense mechanisms may result in avoidance of opposite sex, having only platonic relationships, and not dating. They may reduce the anxiety associated with the drive and satisfy immediate needs but frequent use of these mechanisms may lead to unsatisfactory interpersonal relationships as they stunt personal growth and increase social distance between the individual and others.

Erikson (1968) emphasized the acquisition of ego identity and sense of who and what one is and the cultural determinants of development. He viewed development within a series of psychosocial stages that are in part biologically determined. Associated with each of Erikson's Eight Stages of Development is a crisis, which is simply a psychosocial task that is encountered. Each crisis involves conflict and has two possible outcomes. Erikson believed that there is a disruption of identity during adolescence resulting from both physical and social factors (such as increasing emphasis on making educational decisions and beginning to consider future occupations) that force the adolescent to consider alternatives. He noted the importance of developing a vocational identity and a personal philosophy, which shall provide the adolescent with a reference for evaluating and coping with life events; otherwise, the adolescent may not be capable of forming a coherent and acceptable identity leading to self doubt, role confusion and indulgence in self-destruction activities (e.g., juvenile delinquency or personality aberrations).

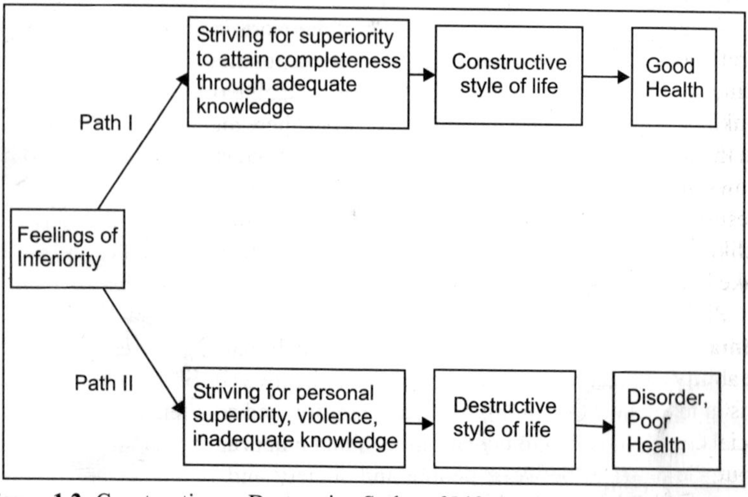

Figure 1.2: Constructive or Destructive Styles of Life Explained by Adler

Adler (1964), the 'Individual Psychologist' mentions styles of life in coping with feelings of inferiority resulting from individual and social development. Adolescence is the most crucial threshold here, forming constructive or destructive styles of life as shown below (Figure 1.2).

Adolescence, takes the centre stage in developing styles of life and physiological changes, being the focal of this stage, demand attention and care. Reproductive health education would carve a responsible adult capable of exercising its rights out of a curious adolescent.

Abraham Maslow (1943), theory of the "self-actualization" is that our needs can be arranged in "a hierarchy ascending from such basic physiological needs as hunger and thirst through safety and love needs to needs for esteem, and ultimately, self-actualization". This hierarchy of needs theory is based on the assumption that all people have the desire to maximize their potential and strive to do what they are capable of doing. Both maximizing potential and striving to find capability are important goals in education. **Maslow** conveyed reproductive decisions as the basic impetus towards a healthy development and motivation to better performance. To make a good decision, the basic requirement is information and education. One fact becomes strikingly clear that every student is different; their living conditions, health, and confidence are a few of the factors that vary dramatically from student to student. However, one commonality can be detected among all students (learners) that they all have needs.

Mead's Study, "Coming of age" on Samoan girls asserts this point. Samoan girls, with informative autonomy and reproductive decisions were better adjusted adults (Mead, 1950).

Piaget (1952) argues that intelligence develops in a series of stages and it reflects the emergence of biological predispositions as well as cultural influences. While a preadolescent is already capable of concrete operational thinking, i.e., thinking about what is real, the "here and now", an adolescent can think about how he/she might be, not just how he/she is. Abstract thinking allows them to consider identity issues such as "who am I?" and answer this question in more concrete terms than just age, name and various likes and dislikes. The adolescent also has thinking skills to weigh alternatives and make long-term plans and commitments.

Piaget's Theory of Intellectual Development is further clarified by **Selman's** Social Cognition Theory (1980), which states that adolescents have the ability to consider not only their own perspectives but also those of others. This is made possible through social cognition and social role taking skills. Social cognition refers to how we think about others and our relation to them, about the relation between people and society and how we infer others' intentions and feelings. However, social role taking skills relate to adolescents' views of the nature of friendships and their view of the social system, which include laws, morality, and importance of mutual consensus.

Social Learning Theory (SLT) posits that environmental agents (parents, teachers, peers) shape (teach) behaviour both by directly reinforcing desired behaviour and by providing models of socially appropriate behaviour. Bandura (1969, 1973) outlined the basis for Social Learning Theory (SLT) and in conjunction with Walters (1963) discussed Social Learning Theory (SLT) as it relates to adolescent development. By observing a model, the adolescent may learn an entirely new behaviour, e.g., delinquent behaviour (Modeling Effect), while observing a punished/rewarded behaviour of the model inhibits/disinhibits the adolescent from doing an act (Inhibition/Disinhibition Effect). On the other hand, by observing the response to the model, the observer may be cued to demonstrate a similar behaviour, which is already in his/her repertoire (Response-Facilitation Effect).

Social Learning Theory (SLT) does not support the idea that development occurs in a sequence of stages. Adolescent development is seen as a direct consequence of cultural conditioning and social expectations for certain kinds of behaviours. The best way to understand this is to examine the impact of models and the odds of reinforcement on adolescent experiences. Any deviant development is seen as failure of socialization processes that began in childhood. Although individual and biological factors play a role in how one will develop, **Mead** (1950, 1953) argued that development differs from one culture to another because of differences in cultural institutions. Cultural contexts define expected and allowable behaviour of adolescents and they exert a significant impact on the nature of adolescence. In different cultures, psychological and social changes are associated with behavioural expectations and different sanctioned behaviours within cultural contexts.

Adolescence is a time when adolescents can experiment with adult roles and determine a realistic sense of self. Adolescents may not have to accept the degree of responsibility that adults do when they take on various roles. The long-term consequences of trying out a role and having it to fail are not as great as they are for adults. Adolescence can determine the degree to which various social roles and situations are comfortable. It is a time when one may ask the question 'Who am I?' and begin to answer it meaningfully. Adolescence is the period during which the skills and attitudes are acquired to help develop adults who will eventually contribute to society in meaningful ways. Adolescents may obtain the skills and training necessary to prepare them for adult roles. Those who did not acquire these skills at this stage are at a disadvantage in their later life. Society will also suffer if its adult members are not well prepared for their marital, parental and civic roles. For adolescents to reach their greatest possible potential, society must provide the needed support structure such as access to basic education, technical trainings, and health education. The development of society and the individual should be in synchrony; otherwise, it will produce frustration for both the individual and society. In effect, transitions experienced during adolescence will be more difficult.

Adolescence Teachable Moments

Adolescence is taken as a period of teachable moment. The adolescence stage characterized by high motivation to learn and that earlier knowledge lasts in all contexts including sexuality. A number of factors hinder provision of sexual and reproductive health education. Difficulties reported as hindering adolescents' sexual and reproductive health education include the belief by parents that their children are too young to receive such education, the embarrassment felt when talking about the subject, and the belief that it may encourage promiscuity (Kelefang and Lennéer, 2008). A WHO study has shown that education in sexual and reproductive health issues does not lead to young people becoming sexually active. The idea underlying sexual and reproductive health education is that a positive view on sexuality leads to greater self esteem and to the capacity to have control over one's own sexual life (WHO, 1996). There is an openness and shared vision among many people towards sexual and reproductive health education and this is a "most humanistic way to promote sexual and reproductive well-being, health and rights". The most important is a source of information and kind of information that is given if adolescents are to have high sense of self efficacy, and have control of decisions concerning their live.

This crucial stage of development seeks exposure through various conspicuous and inconspicuous sources confiding in peer groups, print media, audio-visual media, book, and so on. Hesitation in seeking answers to the obvious development changes or sudden aggressive, autonomous ways to find answers either results in inadequate development or dangerous outcomes. It is therefore, of utmost importance that the prime socializing agencies namely family and school must provide the required information and understanding. If adolescents successfully resolve the crisis arising due to the physiological and mental changes, they can prove to be a rich human resource for the country.

Almost all the studies stressed on the various needs and concerns of adolescents. It is to be noted that the author can not stress on a single theory which explains the need and importance of imparting reproductive health education to adolescents. Depending on various situations of adolescents different theories can become applicable.

Scientific Background

Scientific background has been drawn from the perspective of various psychosocial theories existed in the field of adolescents and adolescence. The theoretical perspective reflected that adolescents physical, cognitive, and emotional development occurs within social institutions, including family, friends, and school. Therefore, understanding the nature of development necessitates understanding the social contexts in which it occurs. For adolescents, families, peers, and schools constitute the most important cultural contexts in which development unfolds.

It is widely accepted that adolescents have the right to reproductive health education, partly because it is a means by which they are helped to protect themselves against abuse, exploitation, unintended pregnancies, sexually transmitted infections and HIV/AIDS. Reproductive health education is the process of acquiring information and training attitudes and beliefs about reproductive health issues. Reproductive health is not limited to the life transmission or reproduction as it includes four important dimensions:

- Anatomy and biology with sex physiology, procreation and survival mankind;
- Social dimension with cultural influence, social norms and rules;
- Psychological dimension with gender issue, the personality construction and self esteem; and
- Affective and relational dimension with feelings (love, desire), points of view and emotions.

Reproductive health education seeks both to reduce the risks of potentially negative outcomes from sexual behaviour like unwanted or unplanned pregnancies and sexually transmitted infections, and to enhance the quality of relationships. It is also about developing adolescents' ability to make decisions over their entire lifetime. It is necessary, in order to go beyond a prescriptive approach, and adopt a decidedly educational perspective. In this way, taking into account adolescent students' representations is an important part of the learning process. The interest of taking them into account in an HIV/AIDS education programme for students has already been underlined (WHO, 1999; WHO, 2006). Reproductive health education requires the teacher and parents representations also so that they could help adolescents build more relevant ones.

Thus there is a need to look at the representations of adolescents', teachers' and parents'. It requires not only to target the knowledge learning but also to take into account the social and cultural aspects.

Rationale of the Study

Adolescence is a vital stage of growth and development. It is a period of transition from childhood to adulthood and is marked by rapid physiological and psychological changes. This period results in sexual, psychological and behavioural maturation. It is an established fact that adolescence is a period of increased risk-taking and therefore susceptible to behavioural problems at the time of puberty and new concerns about reproductive health. Female adolescents, compared to their male counterparts, face disproportionate health concerns following puberty, foremost among these are too-early pregnancy and frequent childbearing. Male adolescents, for their part, often lack a sense of shared responsibility for reproductive matters and respect for reproductive choices there is a growing acceptance of the fact that adolescents need information and education so that they can protect themselves and make informed decisions regarding their reproductive health. At the same time it is acknowledged that parents have important roles and responsibilities in that context. Despite such awareness, resistance persists. Some myths prevail that educating adolescents about reproductive health and providing them with related information and services will lead to irresponsibility and promiscuity, although studies have shown that the reverse is true. For their part, many adolescents are reluctant to seek help from adults either within their families or in school they therefore do not get the information, counseling and services they need. There is a need of involving parents and of fostering an "enabling environment by equipping adults, through training and sensitization efforts, to help adolescents. Adult family members of both sexes have to be informed of the need and value of reproductive health education for adolescents, and need to be reassured that young people need their support. Thus parents ought to be the main source of information on reproductive health education but are not giving adolescents what they needed.

It has been recognized that the efficient way to reach young people and their families are through schools. Teachers can function as healthy role models, advocates for healthy school environments, gatekeepers for students in need of services, resource people for accurate information and effective instructions. Schools could provide a safe place for adolescents to discuss reproductive health issues, get advice and explore non-stereotypical gender roles. However, little is known about how prepared schools are to embark in the task of reproductive health education.

In the above context, the study looks after the adolescents' reproductive health issues, including the knowledge, perception and context within which they arise and also explored the opinion of parents and teachers on imparting reproductive health education amongst adolescents. An attempt is also made to study the existing policies and programmes with respect to reproductive health education for adolescents.

Relevance to Social Work Practice

This research would help the social workers in understanding the issues related to the reproductive health of adolescents. It would help in raising the sensitization among social workers about the different problems encountered by adolescents in the getting information on reproductive health issues. It would highlight the need to make the existing school health service more sensitive to the needs of adolescents. This would enable the social work professionals to bridge the gap between the adolescents and adults (parents and teachers) who continue to be the main and easily accessible source of information especially in the area of reproductive health education for adolescents.

The study would help in promoting health related research with specific reference to reproductive health of adolescents. Further there is a need that the information regarding reproductive health issues should be made available to adolescents, so that they can make informed and responsible decisions. It would emphasize on the need to provide education to adolescents and organization working with adolescents to make them aware of their rights and responsibilities for their own personal health care, and to encourage them to demand for reproductive health education that would meet their particular needs and concern.

In order to ensure universal access to reproductive health education for the adolescents the study would emphasize on the need to create and support programmes in the schools as well community, also help in realizing the need to create programmes and services that address specific health needs of adolescents.

Objectives

1. To study government policies and programmes with respect to reproductive health education for adolescents.
2. To examine the knowledge and perception of adolescent students of government and private schools regarding reproductive health issues.
3. To identify the various sources of information accessed by the students about reproductive health issues.
4. To examine the opinion of parents about need of imparting reproductive health education to the adolescents.
5. To examine the opinion of teachers about need of imparting reproductive health education to the adolescents.
6. To suggest social work interventions in order to impart appropriate knowledge and attitude among adolescents regarding reproductive health issues.

Methodology

In order to accomplish the objective of the study, approach to triangulation of both qualitative and quantitative research methods was adopted. The design of the study was descriptive. The present research described various aspects of adolescents' reproductive health. The study described the status of reproductive health education as it exists in schools, role of parents and teachers in imparting reproductive health education amongst adolescents, in order to suggest suitable social work interventions. The universe comprised of all the school going adolescents in senior classes (9th-12th class) in the National Capital Territory of Delhi. It also included all the parents and teachers of these adolescents. The Probability sampling method was used to draw the required sample of adolescent students. It was done by using Multi Stage Stratified Random sampling technique. The sample size consisted of 320 students i.e., 160 students (80 girls and 80 boys) from each stratum (government and private schools). The sampling procedure involved the following steps:

- In the first stage a list of all the schools providing secondary level education in Delhi was obtained from Directorate of Education. Based on this list schools were categorized as government schools and private schools. From each stratum, equal number of schools i.e. four schools were selected using random number tables.
- The second stage comprised of comprehensive source lists of all the students studying in different sections between 9th -12th classes in the selected schools. This was resulted in four strata for the purpose of present study.
- Finally in the third stage, a sample of 20 students was selected using systematic sampling from each stratum (9th, 10th, 11th, and 12th). Thus the total number of students selected from one school was 80, thereby bringing the total sample size of students to 320. Care was taken to give equal representation to males and females. There was also a back up sample of 10 students from each school (in case of non availability of selected students).

A sample of parents and teachers was selected by using Non- Probability Method of Purposive Sampling. Total sample size was 40 teachers and 40 parents. The data was collected using self - administered inventory with the adolescents and interview guide with the parents and teachers. The tools were thoroughly pre-tested before formal data collection process for fine-tuning of self administered inventory as well as interview guide. Pre-testing really helped the author to make the study realistic and meaningful; it also helped the author to get acquainted to the situations prevailing in the schools in context of reproductive health education. The author found the process of writing field notes productive, not just of description but of first reflections on connections between expressions and feelings of adolescent students and their teachers and parents with regards to reproductive health issues. Both verbal and non-verbal expressions of respondents have been taken in the field diary and used in further chapters. Secondary data was also collected through internal as well external sources. Both qualitative and quantitative analysis of data has been done.

Inclusion Criteria

- Adolescent students: The student studying between classes IX- XII in a co-educational government or private school in the National Capital Territory of Delhi and were willing to participate in the research.
- Parents: Only those parents formed a part of research whose children were studying between class IX-XII in a co-educational government or private school In the National Capital Territory of Delhi and willing to participate in research.
- Teachers: The teacher teaching any of the classes between class IX-XII of a co-educational government or private school in the National Capital Territory of Delhi and were willing to participate in the research.

Ethical Considerations

Permission to carry out the research was obtained from the principals of the schools involved. (Principals have the authority to allow cross sectional studies to be conducted without parental consent in India.) This complies with the Helsinki Declaration for research conducted with humans. All participants provided written consent prior to being involved in the research and all results were de-identified prior to reporting.

Field Work: Process

Field work period for the research was from January 2009, to October, 2009. To begin with data collection, the following procedure was followed.

- First of all a comprehensive list of the schools to be visited (area wise) was identified.
- Then the researcher met the Principals of the concerned schools and took necessary permissions but few Principals were apprehensive and reluctant to give permission for interviewing the target group. But when they were explained about the purpose of the research and that it would not cause them any problems, then gradually they opened up and granted permission. Also the school

timings were noted down and list of students studying there obtained.

- The researcher also enquired with the Principals about the convenient timings when the data could be collected so as not to disturb the routine activities at school.
- At a time, a particular school was selected and after necessary permissions were obtained the interviews were conducted within the school premises itself.
- A self administered, English language (at the secondary level all students can read and write basic English) inventory comprising both multiple-choice and descriptive questions was developed. As the research covered sensitive issues, and to avoid confounding through discussion amongst participants, data were collected on the same day in each school. There were no refusals. At the beginning of each session, an information statement was read to students outlining the aim of the research and the reason respondents had been selected. Students were instructed to place their completing self administered inventory into the envelope provided.
- Parents were interviewed on the day of PTM (Parent Teachers meeting). Permission was also taken from the parents to interview them on the day of PTM (Parent Teachers meeting)
- Interview of teachers were conducted at the school premises itself during their rest/free periods.

Processing, Analysis and Interpretation of Data

Both quantitative and qualitative analysis of data has been done. In quantitative analysis, the data was tabulated and analyzed using the statistical analysis software package (SPSS 14.0 for Windows Evaluation Version). Frequencies were assessed for each question. The descriptive statistics included mean of the data pertaining to specific variables. The nature of distribution of variables taken in the research was assessed from the bi-variate and tri-variarte tables obtained. Graphical Analysis i.e. graphs, bar diagrams and pie- diagrams were prepared to provide a more appropriate interpretation of the processed data. Chi-square could not be applied as the number of frequencies in some of the cell was less than 5 in majority of the tables.

In qualitative analysis, transcripts of the interview were prepared and organized according to the analytical headings. Information was taken from the transcripts and the respondents accounts were organized by the themes and subcategories. These themes were developed from the literature, discussion with key informants and emerged from the analysis of transcripts. The data included in each heading reflected the range of views on particular issues.

2

Reproductive Health Education for Adolescents: An Appraisal

Reproductive health is an important component of overall health and well-being. It is a major, positive part of personal health and healthy living and it follows that "reproductive health education should be available to all as an important component of health promotion and services" (UN, 1994). Providing reproductive health education in school is nowadays an important public health issue, as it concerns not only prevention of adolescents from HIV/AIDS, sexually transmitted infections, and pregnancy but also interpersonal relationships and psychosocial issues. Therefore providing reproductive health education in school contributes to promote better citizenship. The reproductive health issues covered by the studies reviewed here are on various aspects of adolescents reproductive health viz., physical and psychological development during adolescence, reproductive and sexual health and interpersonal relationships between adolescents and parents, members of the opposite sex, peer group, gender roles in respect of reproductive and sexual health issues, importance of socio cultural norms of sexual behaviour and healthy attitude towards the opposite sex, need for adolescent health services, adolescent pregnancy and its consequences, unsafe abortion, adolescents myths and misconceptions, sexual abuse, STIs, HIV/ AIDS, and substance abuse and its relationship to other high risk behaviours.

The Scope

The chapter presents fifty six (In order to bring more clarity one study is reviewed under many themes and sub-themes according to the findings of that study) studies which described the various dimensions involved in imparting reproductive health education for adolescents. For obtaining relevant information on reproductive health education, literature on empirical studies, articles and books has been thematically reviewed under five themes according to the objectives of the present study. Each study further reviewed under various sub-themes according to the themes emerging from a particular study.

Knowledge and Perception of Adolescents regarding Reproductive Health Issues

This section is further divided into ten sub-themes as dealt hereunder:

- Process of growing up
- Age at Marriage
- Adolescent pregnancy and its consequences
- Unsafe abortion
- Contraception
- Sexual behaviour
- Sexual abuse
- STI/HIV/AIDS
- HIV/AIDS related knowledge
- Substance abuse

Process of Growing up

Understanding the reproductive health needs of adolescents, both physical and emotional, is crucial for their health and well-being. Against this backdrop, to understand the process of growing up, nine studies were reviewed in this section.

Ahuja and Tewari (1995) have conducted a study titled "awareness of pubertal changes among adolescent girls" aiming to determine the awareness among adolescent girls regarding the changes that occur during puberty, their beliefs and practices relating to menstruation, their main sources of information on these issues and their exposure to sex education. The sample comprised adolescent girls (50 school going and 50 non-schools going) in the age group of 12-16 years. A questionnaire and personal interviews were used as tools to gather data. Findings show that the girls were aware of pubertal changes and the onset of the menstrual cycle during adolescence. But about three fourth of them were unaware of the physiology of menstruation and experienced a sense of isolation during their periods.

Sharma and Sharma (1995) have conducted a study titled "The letter-box approach- A model for sex education in an orthodox society" A community survey conducted to study the sexual behaviour of adolescent boys and girls in ten villages in kheda district of Gujarat. In an attempt to impart sex education in an acceptable manner, a letter-box approach was developed, assuring anonymity to the students. Teachers were recruited to impart knowledge to the children, as parents were most reluctant to do so. Very few teachers volunteered because they themselves had a lot of misconceptions and confusion about sexuality. After a letter-box was installed inside the college/school campus, the students were encouraged to drop letters into the box with queries about various health-related problems and those related to their bodies. The response was heartening. Most of the questions asked by the boys were related to masturbation and the size of the penis, and by girls about menstruation, body hair, and the size of the breasts. The advantage of this model was that it made use of a group/team approach, which gave confidence to the teachers as well as the students

Khan *et al.*, (1996) in the research titled "Knowledge, attitude and sexual behaviour of school going adolescents in Uttar Pradesh" assessed adolescents' awareness of reproductive physiology, family planning, and AIDS/STD. An attempt was also made to analyze their sexual behaviour. The study was carried out in eight schools of Lucknow city, four private English medium schools, and four government public schools. A total of 510 students (270 boys and 240 girls) were systematically selected after a random start. A structured questionnaire was administered to collect relevant information. Two thirds of the students were 16-18 years, one-third was 15 years or less, and four students were 19 years old. Demographic and socio-economic analysis did not show any significant differences between boys and girls, but a major economic disparity was revealed between the students studying in government and private schools. In the study the level of knowledge about reproductive physiology revealed a general lack of awareness, although private school students were better informed than their counterparts in public schools.

Sharma and Sharma (1996) undertook a study titled "Sexual knowledge and practices of college girls in rural Gujarat" to determine the knowledge of human sexuality, physiology of reproduction, and contraception among adolescent girls. The influence of various demographic and socio-cultural factors such as parental education and socio-economic background on the level of awareness in adolescents was also assessed. Unmarried girls (N=530) with a science background studying in the first year of college (mean age = 17.3 years) participated in the study. Data were collected with a pre-tested questionnaire assessing the variables mentioned. ANOVA and multiple regression analysis revealed that (1) overall knowledge about human sexuality, reproduction, and contraception was poor among the college girls; (2) knowledge scores were significantly higher among girls who had educated parents and had learnt about sexuality from their elders (elder siblings, teachers, and in some cases parents); (3) girls residing in hostels had a higher level of awareness than girls living with their parents; and (4) a history of masturbation was found to be positively associated with knowledge regarding sexuality.

Shilpa and Ratna Kumari (1999) in their study titled "Knowledge of high school students on reproductive health and AIDS" examined the knowledge of students (class IXth and Xth) on reproductive health and AIDS and gender differences. The sample consisted of 200 boys and 200 girls (12-16 years). A questionnaire was used to assess the knowledge on reproductive health and HIV/AIDS. The study found that the majority of the students lacked knowledge regarding various aspects of reproductive health, indicators of physical maturity in girls and boys', indicators of pregnancy and family planning methods.

Yadav (2003) conducted a study on Awareness and Attitude of adolescent students towards reproductive health issues in different cultural settings, i.e., Rural, urban and tribal. Sample of the study comprised the students of IX class of Madhya Pradesh. Questionnaire consisted of 16 items, awareness test of 3 parts having items Yes/No/Do not know and of multiple choices, Attitude scale- 60 statements on 3-point scales- Agree/Disagree/Not Sure was used as tool of data collection. The study has highlighted that students have low awareness about various aspects of physiological and psychological development. Students either wrongly reported or were not aware about issues related to growing up aspects, health, pregnancy, and interpersonal relationships.

Dash (2004) in the research titled "reproductive health problems of unmarried adolescent girls" assessed their level of knowledge about reproductive health problems. Sample size of 100 girls selected from sample frame of 663 girls in 10 villages. All enumerated girls were arranged village wise. Systematic random sampling with a random start method was used. Interview schedule was used as a tool to gather the data. The study threw light on the fact of sanitation and hygienic condition during menses, it was found that during menses, girls used old clothes and reuse the same after wash. Causes and consequences of reproductive health problems were low.

Sahoo (2004) in his study titled "level of knowledge on sexual health education among unmarried adolescents" found that knowledge about menstrual health was poor among adolescent girls. The sample comprised of 100 adolescents (55 male and 45 female) selected using simple random method. An interview schedule contained questions related to the socio-economic status and knowledge regarding sexual and reproductive health was administered. Respondents pointed out that parents and guardian were main obstacles to gain knowledge on reproductive and sexual health.

Prasad (2006) conducted a study titled "Perception on Sexual Matters among Rural Adolescent Boys: A study in Andhra Pradesh". The objectives of the study were to understand the sexuality among adolescent boys, and to throw light on Hindu and Muslim rural adolescent boys' awareness regarding perception on sexual matters. A pre-designed questionnaire was administered on 200 Hindu and 200 Muslim adolescent boys. It was reported by the study that a significant proportion of adolescent boys did not answer about masturbation, bed-wetting or erection. The study reflected that misconceptions regarding masturbation and extra-marital relations needs to be cleared up.

Age at Marriage

This section dealt with the studies related to age at marriage. Five studies were reviewed in this section.

The study conducted by Uplaonkar (1995) titled "The emerging rural youth: A study of their changing values towards marriage" aimed to analyze whether youth have emerged as a distinct group anchored by the modern values of freedom and autonomy, able to decide the issues of life completely on their own. The objectives of the study were to know values of youth towards ideal age at marriage for males and females, and the choice of a life partner. The major findings are: (1) Eighty-five percent of the respondents indicated 21-25 years as the optimal age for males. Age range indicated for females was 17-18 years. (2) In choosing a life partner, the youth want a certain amount of autonomy in conformity with the ideas of the joint family. (3) A considerable percentage of rural youth wanted to exercise an independent choice, in consultation with their parents. In comparison with men, however women were more tradition bound; ninety eight percent opted for partner selection by parents only.

The study carried out by Gupta and Khan (1996) looked at the fertility differentials among adolescents (13-19 years of age) and currently married women in Uttar Pradesh (UP) and tries to determine whether regional/district level variations exist in these differentials. Results regarding teenage girls revealed: (i) A significant difference in the proportion of married teenage girls by residence (urban/rural), educational level, religion, and caste groups. In six out of the 15 surveyed districts, about 25 per cent of all adolescent girls were married. (ii) Age at marriage was high in western and hill regions, whereas it was low in central, eastern, and Bundelkhand regions. (iii) A positive correlation (0.76) between female literacy and the mean age at marriage was seen. (iv) A negative correlation (-0.80) between the percentage married and the mean age at marriage was observed. (v) Awareness of family planning was quite high among teenage wives, although lower than that among the older couples (> 20 years). (vi) The contribution of teenage fertility to the total fertility rate (TFR) was around 15 per cent with wide regional variations. (vii) Regional variations were also quite large, with the eastern region displaying the highest unmet need for child spacing among the teenage respondents.

Umamani and Raju (1997) revealed that many females get married at an early age in India. This is of concern because early marriages raise the level of fertility and maternal and child mortality, lower the level of literacy, and increase the chance of a wide age gap between the spouses. The sample of the study comprised of currently married women (N=644) in the age group of 15-49 Years from Mandya district of Karnataka state. The Census studies regarding the Mandya district indicated that the females married earlier in the district than in the state (Karnataka). The cultural practice of pre puberty marriages was also reported in the district. The results, analyzed using regression analysis and Multiple Correlation Analysis, confirmed the practice of pre puberty marriages among the present sample due to various factors such as caste, consanguinity, and illiteracy. The percentage of pre puberty marriages was significantly higher amongst the scheduled castes than amongst the Vokkaligas (a caste group in Mandya district). The marriages were also significantly more common amongst close relatives than non-relatives and amongst the illiterates than the literate groups.

Shilpa and Ratnakumari (1999) in their study titled "Knowledge of high school students on reproductive health and AIDS" found that a high percentage of students (class IXth and Xth) were aware of the appropriate age of marriage.

The study conducted by George (2004) determined the level of knowledge and attitude of adolescents regarding select reproductive health issues. Sample of 120 adolescents was selected out of 295 in the age group of 11-19 years. 50 percent sample of 8 villages was selected by simple random sampling from the list of 15 villages arranged geographically. An interview schedule was used as a tool for data collection. The findings of the study reflect that seventy four per cent adolescents were aware of the fact that the girls could get married at eighteen years or above.

Adolescent Pregnancy and its Consequences

Pregnancy at any age generates developmental changes, but in an adolescent it can create a developmental crisis. Failure to accomplish developmental tasks not only places the adolescent at risk for further developmental difficulties, but it places the children of these adolescents at biological, social, and psychological risk. In this section six studies were reviewed.

The study conducted by Ahuja and Tiwari (1995) with the adolescents in the age group of 12-16 years showed that very few of the students knew the appropriate age for marriage and childbearing, and 80 per cent reported no exposure to sex or health education.

The review of studies by Kamat (1996) highlights major issues related to the risk factors influencing teenage pregnancy and its outcomes. The risk factors are presented under three main headings: (1) Nutrition: Chronic under-nutrition during childhood or before/during pregnancy and inadequate weight gain during pregnancy lead to negative outcomes like low birth weight (LBW) infants, pre-term delivery, etc. Anemic adult women also undergo undesirable pregnancy outcomes. (2) Physical and clinical: Early age of menarche results in various undesirable pregnancy outcomes. Even at late age of menarche, the relationship between low gynecological age and poor pregnancy outcome remains controversial. Adequacy of antenatal care is significantly associated with pregnancy outcomes of adolescent mothers, more in the developing countries. (3) Socio-economic: Female illiteracy and ignorance, widespread in socio-economically deprived communities, not only contribute to undesirable pregnancy outcomes, but also pose difficulty for studies in obtaining reliable information on factors like maternal age, age at menarche, prenatal weight gain, etc. At a broader level, teenage pregnancy is a burden on the national economy and adversely affects national family planning programmes. Interaction of the combined effects of various factors on pregnancy outcomes related to the nutritional and socio-economic status of the mother needs to be investigated.

The study done by Pratinidhi (1996) was based on observations of adolescent pregnancy during a community-based research project. For teenage pregnancy, nutritional advice and referral to health center/hospital for delivery were considered adequate intervention. It was found that: (1) 10 percent of the total deliveries were to women less than 20 years old and the children of these mothers faced the highest perinatal and neonatal mortality, (2) mothers below 18 years of age also faced greater risks of primiparity and associated factors like prolonged labour, short stature, and anemia when compared to other women, (3) babies born to primipara mothers below 18 years suffered higher rates of perinatal and neonatal mortality, alongwith additional risks, (4) comparing the proportion of primigravida women below 18 years in this study with an earlier study on the same population of Sirur, there was a declining trend in pregnancy below 18 years, (5) a significantly higher proportion of low birth weight babies and anemic mothers in the high risk group was explained by malnutrition, (6) the ignorance and immaturity of mothers were largely responsible for higher morbidity and mortality among adolescent mothers themselves and babies born to them.

In the study conducted by Atwood and Hussein (1997) adolescent motherhood has been discussed in the light of a large proportion of girls in India marrying under the age of 18. The researchers discussed the various factors that contribute towards making adolescent girls particularly vulnerable to early marriage and motherhood in rural India. The girls undergo a premature transition to adult roles due to early responsibility for domestic roles, poverty, illiteracy, and poor nutrition. Although the scenario is marginally different for the urban girls, there is greater concern to study the situation of their rural counterparts, because most adolescent girls live in rural areas and form a large and neglected group. Early marriage and childbearing (15-19 age group) may lead to higher mortality rates, because the girls have not attained complete physical maturity. The consequent effects on the newborn, such as higher perinatal and neonatal mortality, stunting, reduced immunity, and reduced learning ability, are discussed. Under these grim circumstances, Atwood and Hussein (1997) discussed on developing a multidisciplinary approach to understand the factors leading to adolescent motherhood.

George (2004) has revealed in the study on knowledge and attitude related to reproductive health of adolescents, that thirty seven per cent of adolescent boys were aware that girls can become pregnant the very first time she had sex with a person as compared to eighty three per cent of adolescent girls aware of the same. Twenty four percent of boys were aware as against forty nine per cent of girls that even if a girl washed her vagina after sex that she could become pregnant.

It was identified by the study conducted by Sahoo (2004) on the "level of knowledge on sexual health education among unmarried adolescents" that knowledge about consequence of early pregnancy was poor among unmarried adolescents.

Unsafe Abortion

Seven studies were reviewed in this section related to unsafe abortion. As abortion is such a sensitive topic, levels of induced abortion are difficult to measure directly.

Thapa and Rawal (1998) summarized information available from various surveys regarding the prevalence of premarital sexual experience among teenage boys and girls in different regions of India. They reported that of the 110 abortions done every month in a medical college in Thiruvananthapuram, 12 per cent were to unmarried teenagers. According to the Ministry of Health, in Maharashtra 21.7 percent of all abortions done were for girls younger than 15 years of age.

United Nations Population Fund (UNFPA) (1998) provided a composite picture of adolescents in the SAARC countries on three major areas: (1) demographic and socioeconomic profile; (2) marriage and childbirth; and (3) sexual and reproductive health status. The statistics indicated the following: Although 60 percent of the region's adolescents are literate, indicating improvements in educational opportunities, there is wide disparity among the SAARC countries (90% in Srilanka and Maldives, 32% in Bangladesh). Most did not complete primary school, and the majority did not go to secondary schools (the ratio of Female/Male is 75-100 at the primary and 29-110 at the secondary level). South-Asian girls still marry early and become mothers before they are 18 years old. The percentage of seeking antenatal care- is low, and only a small percentage of babies are delivered by trained birth attendants, in which 11 percent in Bangladesh, Nepal, and Pakistan, and 24 percent in India.

A review of literature conducted by Center for Operations Research and Training (CORT) (1999) highlighted the disadvantaged position of adolescent girls in the prevalence, of malnourishment and anemia, early marriage; high illiteracy, unsafe abortions, poor knowledge of reproductive health and prevention of STD/HIV/AIDS.

Ganatra (2000) conducted a review on abortion related studies. Studies suggested that a substantial proportion of adolescents, both married and unmarried seek abortion services. It is estimated that between 1 and 10 per cent of abortion-seekers in India are adolescents, though a few facility based studies report that the proportion of adolescent abortion-seekers is as high as one in three.

Jejeebhoy (2000) in his study found that among unmarried abortion-seekers, adolescents constituted a disproportionately large percentage. At least one-half of unmarried women seeking abortions were adolescents, many of whom were below 15 years.

Ganatra and Hirve (2002) conducted a community-based study in rural Maharashtra. The study reported that young women aged 15-24 constituted over half of married abortion-seekers in the area. Findings of this study suggested that adolescents have considerably less decision-making authority than older abortion seekers, are more likely to be coerced into an abortion, or conversely, to face opposition from their families, and are more likely to report post-abortion morbidity.

It was indicated by the study done by Sahoo (2004) that knowledge about the reasons and consequences of reproductive health problem were superficial, knowledge about unsafe abortion was very low among adolescents.

Contraception

Adolescents, especially those unmarried, seldom use contraception. Sexually active adolescents who have sex with a steady partner often claim that intercourse is not the result of premeditated or conscious decisions but just "happens", so they are unlikely to be prepared with contraception (Khisbiyah *et al.*, 1997). Five studies were reviewed in this section.

Khan *et al.*, (1996) in a study conducted with school going adolescents assessed their awareness of reproductive physiology, family planning, and AIDS/STI. An attempt was also made to analyze their sexual behaviour. It was found that the awareness of family planning methods was not uncommon among adolescents. More than half of the students (65% male and 43% female) were aware of safe sex.

Analysis of the study conducted by Sharma and Sharma (1996) revealed that: (1) overall knowledge about human sexuality, reproduction, and contraception was poor among the college girls; (2) knowledge scores were significantly higher among girls who had educated parents and had learnt about sexuality from their elders (elder siblings, teachers, and in some cases parents); (3) girls residing in hostels had a higher level of awareness than girls living with their parents. The researchers discussed the need for incorporating family life education in school curricula and the crucial role that teachers can play in bringing about desirable and socially acceptable changes about sexuality and related topics.

UNFPA (1998) in a study on sexual and reproductive health status of adolescents revealed that the use of contraception is low, resulting in adolescent unplanned pregnancies with short spacing. There is a high incidence of reproductive tract infections. Although sex outside marriage is considered taboo, study indicated that adolescents (60% in Bangladesh, 25% in India) do engage in pre-marital sex, raising the risk of unwanted pregnancy and illegal abortion.

Bhatia and Swami (2000) Giving statistical details regarding the increasing population of India and the need to generate awareness particularly in the youth, the study found the level of awareness among girl students in Chandigarh regarding fertility control measures. A majority of the girls were aware of fertility control methods; the level of knowledge regarding fertility control methods increased with age; literacy status of mothers positively influenced the level of knowledge of girls; girls having working mothers and whose fathers were in government and affiliated jobs had a higher level of knowledge than girls whose mothers were housewives; and the girls in rural areas had much lower levels of awareness regarding fertility control methods than their urban counterparts.

George (2004) determined the level of knowledge and attitude of adolescents regarding select reproductive health issues. The study revealed that sixty seven per cent of the boys had a correct understanding of what family planning was whereas only forty five per cent of the girls knew what it is. Most of the boys and girls were in favour of small family norms. Fifty four per cent of the boys say that women should not use family planning services before first delivery whereas sixty three per cent of the girls disagreed to the same.

Sexual Behaviour

As already discussed in the previous section that sex outside marriage is considered taboo, but studies indicated that adolescents do engage in pre-marital sex, raising the risk of unwanted pregnancy and illegal abortion (UNFPA, 1998; Gantara, 2000). In this section twelve studies were reviewed.

Sharma and Sharma (1995) threw a light on the fact that most of the boys had their first sexual contact with a prostitute and had never used a condom. Some of them reported having their first sexual contact with a girl friend of almost the same age. This again brought the light to the fact that some of the unmarried adolescent girls might also be sexually active.

Khan *et al.,* (1996) in his study found that one third of the students favoured premarital sex. Boys indicated a more liberal attitude than girls. It is interesting to note that students of private schools appeared less liberal towards premarital or extra-marital sex than students from public schools.

Jejeebhoy (1996) found that adolescent marriage and fertility rates are disturbingly high; adolescents face a variety of reproductive health problems; evidence suggests 20-30 per cent of males, and up to 10 per cent of females, are sexually active during adolescence before marriage; sexual awareness seems to be largely superficial; double standards exist (favouring boys) for boys and girls; and both married and unmarried women are vulnerable to being unprotected from pregnancy and STDs, and have no decision-making power in their sexual relationships

The study titled "Understanding youth sexuality: A study of college students in Mumbai" conducted by Abraham (1998) provides insights into the sexuality of youth and ascertains knowledge and perception regarding reproductive physiology, STDs, and contraception. The study found that boys were sexually active whereas girls reported low rates of sexual activity. Myths and misconceptions regarding anatomy, physiology, contraceptives, and STDs were prevalent. Sexual activity increased with age, work status, and peer socialization. Religion, family, and educational institutions had limited influence on morality and regulation of sexuality among males, who explored their sexuality through multiple partners more than females.

Awasthi and Pande (1998) found that among the unmarried boys, eight per cent of the boys under 18 years and equal per cent of the boys above 18 years were sexually active and engaged in high risk sexual behaviour (man to man sex, visits to commercial sex workers).

The research done by Chaudhary (1998) revealed some significant emerging trends and myths related to adolescents sexual and reproductive behaviour and underlined the gravity, diversity, and magnitude of the changes taking place in the lives of the adolescents, and brought out the implications of these changes in their lives. The changes ranged from the share of adolescents in the total population to their sexual and reproductive behaviour, social values about sex, marriage and marriage practices, and increasing exposure to STDs, HIV/AIDS, drug abuse, and various forms of sexual exploitation associated with rising industrialization and urbanization. The study identifies evolving gender relations among adolescents and their perspectives and expectations; and it reveals the information and the lack of understanding of the socio cultural context within which the adolescents operate and interact.

Sachdev (1998) in a study of sample comprised of 887 students (19-24 years) from two major universities in Delhi responded to a 30-item inventory regarding male and female sexual anatomy and function, contraception, reproduction and menopause, and common sexual problems. The women respondents expressed liberal views regarding premarital sex and chastity, though they were more conservative than male respondents; e.g., 58 per cent of the female students endorsed premarital sex compared to 79 per cent of males. Female sexuality was acknowledged and opinions favoured fidelity in marriage.

Abraham and Kumar (1999) in their study explored heterosexual behaviour, the findings showed that the majority of males (70%) and females (66%) hold moderate views towards sex in general. Attitudes towards premarital sex differed considerably by gender. 47 per cent of male participants and 13 per cent of females had had sexual experiences, as well as intercourse. Age, year in school, and academic programme significantly influenced the likelihood of females having had sexual experience. Socio-economic variables at the household level did not show any significant relationship with students' sexual behaviour. The study also showed an inconsistent relationship between knowledge about sexual issues and sexual behaviour. The researchers concluded that education programmes on sexuality should be designed to reach out to the students.

While the study by Dash (2004) revealed that ten per cent unmarried girls had sexual experience, of whom majority of them were coerced into sex.

George (2004) found that most of the adolescents of various economic classes were of the opinion that it was not all right to have friends of the opposite sex.

Sahoo (2004) assessed the level of Knowledge on Sexual Health Education among Unmarried Adolescents. He found that Minority (25%) had knowledge about consequences of pre-marital sex.

Study conducted by Prasad (2006) found that eighty six per cent of the adolescent boys opined pre-marital sex is bad. The study also reflected that thirty eight per cent Muslim adolescent boys said extra marital sex was bad.

Sexual Abuse

Only a single study was found by the present research on sexual abuse in the studies related to reproductive health issues. Almost all the studies reviewed here did not concentrate on the sensitive issue of sexual abuse, which is a part of reproductive health education.

A study conducted by McCabe (1996) titled "Sex education programmes for people with mental retardation" indicated that adolescents need special help if they are to acquire socially appropriate sexual behaviour, to make safe sexual choices, and to become less vulnerable to sexual abuse.

STI/ HIV/AIDS

The National Behavioural Surveillance Survey of the National AIDS Control Organisation (NACO) indicates that approximately 3 per cent of young males and 5 per cent of young females (NACO) reported the experience of symptoms of infection (STIs) such as discharge, ulcers or sores in the 12 months preceding the survey. These figures undoubtedly reflect considerable under-reporting (NACO and UNICEF, 2002). In this section ten studies were reviewed.

Sharma and Sharma (1997) conducted a study in Anand Taluka of Gujarat State to assess the sexual behaviour of unmarried, sexually active adolescent boys and to evaluate their knowledge of AIDS and other sexually transmitted diseases (STDs) and of correct use of condoms. A large number of boys believed that STDs were caused by having sexual intercourse with a woman during her menstrual period. It was also commonly believed that STDs could be cured by having sex with a virgin. The boys usually selected a prostitute as the first sexual partner, and this selection was influenced by their employment status, age at first coitus, and literacy level. A majority of the boys believed that HIV infection and AIDS are associated with homosexuality and that, being heterosexuals, they were protected from these diseases. It can be concluded that the sexually active adolescent boys are inadequately prepared to protect themselves against STDs and hence there is a need to impart knowledge of safe sex to them.

Abraham (1998) reflected on a very important finding that the risk of STDs/HIV was high among males because they practiced unsafe sex and among females because of ignorance. Information about behaviour, attitudes, and knowledge through regular surveys is essential to better understand the dynamics of the STI epidemic. This information is also important in assessing changes over time as a result of prevention efforts.

The study by Awasthi and Pande (1998) assessed the sexual behaviour patterns and knowledge of STD among underprivileged 15-21-year-old boys. The adolescents had poor knowledge regarding STD prevention, placing them' at high risk for STD/HIV.

Harms *et al.*, (1998) study titled "Perceptions and patterns of reproductive tract infections in a young rural population in Namibia" found the causes of the increased rates of STIs/HIV in young people are complex, however, the main reasons include biological factors, risky sexual behaviour patterns (early initiation of sex, premarital sex, bisexual orientation and multiple sexual partners), transmission dynamics and treatment-seeking behaviour.

Dash (2004) revealed in his study that causes and consequences of reproductive health was low, nearly half of the girls were not aware of hazards of unsafe abortion, knowledge of RTI/STI was low.

While a study conducted by Sahoo (2004) found that few of the respondents had knowledge about STD. Knowledge of HIV was better (60%).

A study conducted by UNFPA (1998) indicated that there is growing evidence of increased premarital sexual activities among young people. While generalization is difficult, study indicates that between 20 per cent and 30 per cent of young men and up to 10 per cent of young women have premarital sexual experiences. Women, have a higher incidence of STIs than men because of their greater biological susceptibility.

NACO, MOHFW, and GOI (2005) revealed that Sexually Transmitted Infections (STI's), including HIV (Human Immunodeficiency Virus) mainly affects sexually active young people. Young adults aged 15–29 years, account for thirty per cent of AIDS (Acquired Immunodeficiency Syndrome) cases reported in India and the number of young women living with HIV/AIDS is twice that of young men.

The findings of the study titled "Study of knowledge, perception and attitude of adolescent girls towards STIs/HIV, safer sex and sex education: A cross sectional survey of urban adolescent school girls in South Delhi" by McManus and Dhar (2008) indicated that knowledge about STIs other than HIV/AIDS was very poor among adolescents. The majority (71%) had not heard about Genital Herpes and almost half had not heard about Gonorrhoea (44%) or Syphilis (43%). This is of particular concern in developing countries like India, as STIs such as Chlamydia, Trichomoniasis, Syphilis and Gonorrhea are second only to maternal morbidity and mortality as the cause of death, illness and 'years of healthy life lost' among women in their child bearing years.

HIV/AIDS Related Knowledge

Sixteen studies were reviewed on HIV/AIDS related knowledge.

Study done by Aggarwal and Kumar (1997) evaluated the existing level of knowledge and awareness about AIDS in 9th and 10th class students from rural and urban areas. Results of the study indicated a high level of knowledge about AIDS (36%-59% correct responses) considering the short time span of a campaign against AIDS in India. But misconceptions about transmission, prognosis, and prevention were also present. Rural girls had significantly more knowledge as well as misconceptions regarding AIDS than urban girls. In this study 57 per cent believed that persons with HIV/AIDS could be detected by their physical appearance.

The study by Amalraj *et al.*, (1997) aimed to find out future health care professionals' knowledge of HIV transmission, misconceptions about the route of transmission, the modes of prevention, and knowledge regarding clinical manifestations. The results reflected that ninety-two per cent of the students were aware of AIDS, predominantly through mass media, although misconceptions regarding transmission of HIV existed, more among females than males. Attitudes were generally negative: one fourth said they would not be friends with HIV-infected people, one-fifth were undecided, a little more than half had no objection to such students attending college, but almost 40 per cent felt that physicians with AIDS should not be allowed to work. More male (36%) than female (9%) students admitted practicing safe sex, mainly with friends.

The study by Bahulekar and Garg (1997) assessed AIDS awareness in schoolchildren regarding its cause, mode of transmission, and prevention. Nearly 10 per cent of the students had not heard about HIV or AIDS, 59.8 per cent knew nothing about signs and symptoms, most of them had misconceptions about the mode of transmission, 49.6 per cent were not aware of prevention methods.

Bhasin *et al.*, (1997) conducted a study to find out the existing knowledge and awareness regarding HIV/AIDS amongst schoolchildren, and to find out the impact of information, education, and communication (IEC) on their subsequent knowledge. A post-IEC evaluation was carried out after a gap of 10 days. Results were encouraging regarding the awareness of the general aspects of HIV/AIDS (97.8% of the total participants of this study) and the fact that AIDS occurs in India. IEC intervention was effective in dispelling misconceptions and significantly generated an enhancing effect on most aspects of the subjects' awareness of HIV/AIDS.

The basic objective of the study by Khan and Singh (1997) was to evaluate knowledge, attitudes, and behaviour among groups of college and university students regarding HIV infection. Results cover each of these points. They show that 88 per cent of the students are aware of AIDS but several misconceptions persist. Students opined that counseling was an essential component of management of HIV infection.

The study by Lal *et al.,* (1997) assessed urban students' knowledge, attitudes, and beliefs related to HIV/AIDS and compared them with those of their rural counterparts.

The study conducted by Rahate *et al.,* (1997) was planned to determine how aware young adolescents from rural areas were about AIDS and its risk factors. The sample consisted of 261 students (107 commerce, 82 science, and 72 arts students) from a junior college of rural Saonar, District Nagpur. A questionnaire comprising questions on various aspects of AIDS, such as etiology, high risk groups, mode of transmission, treatment, and methods of prevention, was administered to the subjects, who ranged from 16 to 20 years (59.77% males and 40.23% females). The researchers found poor overall knowledge regarding the etiology of AIDS. About 70-80 per cent of the students were aware of high risk groups and modes of transmission of AIDS, but an equally high percentage (60-70%) harbored misconceptions regarding the same. A variability of knowledge regarding diagnosis, treatment, prevention, and seriousness of AIDS was observed. Science students were more knowledgeable than arts and commerce students.

The study undertaken by Sundar *et al.*, (1997) determined the knowledge of AIDS transmission and prevention among student population. In spite of re-assuringly high levels of awareness regarding sexual transmission of HIV, findings revealed important gaps regarding other modes of transmission and preventive measures. Levels of knowledge were similar in all categories of the sample, but females knew considerably less and had more misconceptions than males.

Tikoo *et al.,* (1997) study presents level of knowledge among adolescent boys and girls regarding human sexuality and AIDS in India. A research instrument consisting of 99 items pertaining to demographics, knowledge, attitudes, and behaviours regarding human sexuality and AIDS was used. The knowledge scale within the questionnaire was subdivided into a reproductive knowledge scale and an AIDS scale. Results showed that the Indian adolescent has a limited knowledge of human sexuality and AIDS. The higher the age and grade, the higher the score, males scored higher than females. The scores of girls and boys who planned to go to university were significantly different from girls who had no plans for university and boys who planned to get a job, respectively.

The main objective of the study by Verma and Pauri (1997) was to assess and compare AIDS awareness among students of a metropolitan city. Findings revealed that 69 per cent of the students had been aware of AIDS for the past three years; only 5 per cent knew of it for over four years. The most important sources of information were foreign magazines (65%) followed by Indian newspapers/ magazines (43%), friends (32%), and TV (15%). A significantly greater proportion of Bombay students cited foreign magazines as an important source of information, whereas Pune students relied on Indian newspapers. No other significant differences were noted between the cities. A large majority from both cities (77% Pune, 78% Bombay) favoured single-partner sex. While a majority did not admit to knowing any intravenous (IV) drug users, a small percentage (9% and 4%) admitted knowing of Intravenous (IV) drug users in their own college and circle of friends respectively. Many students (59%) from Pune (67%) and Bombay (55%) expressed willingness to join the campaign against AIDS.

Awasthi and Pande (1998) found that adolescents are at the maximum risk of HIV infection, and unlike the developed countries where reproductive health counseling is done mainly through the schools, in India a majority of children drop out after primary school.

Shilpa and Ratnakumari (1999) found that even so, a high percentage of students were aware of the appropriate age of marriage, recognized AIDS to be a sexually transmitted disease, were aware of the modes of transmission of AIDS, and considered it to be the most serious health problem of the country.

Ignorance was prevalent regarding the full form of the acronym HIV/AIDS. Girls from girls' schools were less aware than boys from boys' schools regarding the physiology of AIDS. Preventive measures against AIDS listed by students included use of condoms, blood testing in case of transfusion, and avoidance of intravenous drugs. Respondents also felt that medical professionals and caretakers should take care of AIDS patients. Television, followed by doctors and newspapers/magazines, remained the most popular source of information. Students also expressed interest in including HIV/AIDS as one of the topics at the high school level.

The study titled "Impact assessment of school-based sex education programme amongst adolescents" by Thakor and Kumar (2000), in order to cautioning against the rising proportion of youth who test positive for HIV/AIDS, points out that a majority of the youth remain ignorant about human reproduction and sexually transmitted diseases. The knowledge of students (class IXth and Xth) on reproductive health and AIDS and gender differences was examined.

Study carried out by Dash (2004) on unmarried adolescent girls represent that most of them knew what HIV/AIDS is but knowledge about transmission and prevention is low. This is clearly an area that requires attention.

George (2004) found that Ninety one per cent of boys knew about HIV/AIDS where as only Sixty eight per cent of girls were aware of the same. Most of the boys were aware that AIDS was not curable, but among the girls about Thirty per cent were not aware that it was not curable. Sixty eight per cent of the adolescents of younger age group said that faithfulness to one's own partner was important. As age increased only Forty six per cent held the same view.

It was indicated by the study carried out by Sahoo (2004) among unmarried adolescents that majority of the respondents were aware that using condoms and avoiding multiple partners would prevent HIV infection.

Substance Abuse

Only one study related to reproductive health of adolescents concentrated on the issue of substance abuse. Substance abuse is a very significant component of reproductive health education.

Awasthi and Pande (1998) in their study titled "Sexual behaviour patterns and knowledge of sexually transmitted diseases in adolescent boys in urban slums of Lucknow" found that adolescents who smoked or consumed alcohol were more likely to be sexually active before marriage (using the *Crude odd's* ratio). One third of the boys were smokers and 13.1 per cent drank alcohol. The study described the vulnerability of adolescent truck cleaners in relation to HIV and AIDS transmission. Most of them indulged in unprotected sexual intercourse. Abuse of alcohol, tobacco, and opium 'was very common with these adolescents. The researcher concludes that these adolescent truck cleaners were highly susceptible to the contraction and transmission of HIV/AIDS. He recommends specific programmes to educate them and free distribution of condoms.

Above reviewed studies have suggested that the rapid biological changes during puberty may cause embarrassment and even stress for many girls and boys. These negative attitudes are mostly due to inadequate knowledge. Compared to their parents, adolescents today receive better information and less restriction regarding puberty and sexuality; but misinformation is still evident (Ahuja and Tiwari, 1995; Shilpa and Ratnakumari, 1999; Prasad, 2006). Many adolescents are unsure of what is happening to them when they menstruate or have a wet dream (Sharma and Sharma, 1995; Khan et al., 1996; Yadav, 2003; Dash, 2004; Sahoo, 2004). The reasons for menstrual blood and wet dreams are puzzling to them. Menstrual blood is considered as dirty blood, and something dirty must be hidden. Boys feel guilty the first time they experience wet dreams, because they believe that having a sex dream is a sin. These negative attitudes may discourage adolescents from learning more about health aspects of these natural bodily functions (Sharma and Sharma, 1996; Sahoo, 2004; Prasad, 2006).

Studies have reported that majority of the female adolescents are married before the legal minimum age of 18. The various factors identified by the researchers were caste, illiteracy, religion etc. (Gupta and Khan, 1996; Umamani and Raju, 1997). There were many studies which indicated that a number of adolescents were aware of the right age of marriage (Uplaonkar, 1995; Shilpa and Ratnakumari, 1999; George, 2004).

Many researchers have identified a number of factors related to individual behaviour, family and community situations, and cultural pressures that underlie adolescent sexual and contraceptive behaviour, pregnancy, and childbearing (Kamat, 1996; Pratinidhi, 1996; Atwood and Hussein, 1997; Sahoo, 2004). Ethnicity, income, and the family structure children grow up in have an important influence contributing to their risk for adolescent pregnancy (Kamat, 1996; Pratinidhi, 1996). The studies reviewed above identified additional factors considered to influence adolescent sexual risk taking and pregnancy such as age at first intercourse, community environment, intimate relationships, peer environment, and individual characteristics. Researches argued that having more of these factors present in an adolescent's life places him/her at a higher risk for becoming adolescent parent (Kamat, 1996; Atwood and Hussein, 1997).

Almost all the studies have highlighted the fact that a large proportion of the adolescents, both married and unmariied seek abortion services (Thapa and Rawal, 1998; UNFPA, 1998; CORT, 1999; Gantara, 2000; Jejeebhoy,

2000; Gantara and Hirve, 2002; Sahoo, 2004) and many of them faced post-abortion morbidity (CORT, 1999; Gantara and Hirve, 2002; Sahoo, 2004).

Studies reviewed above reflected that significant number of adolescent boys and girls were sexually active before marriage. Boys were engaged in high risk sexual behaviour such as man to man sex, visit to commercial sex workers and girls were coerced into sex. They were vulnerable to have unwanted pregnancy, abortion, STIs/HIV/AIDS (Sharma and Sharma, 1995; Jejeebhoy, 1996; Abraham, 1998; Awasthi and Pande, 1998; Abraham and Kumar, 1999; Dash, 2004). Adolescents had poor knowledge about the consequences of pre-marital sex (Sahoo, 2004). Boys indicated more liberal views towards pre- marital or extra marital sex than females (Khan *et al.*, 1996; Abraham, 1998; Sachdev, 1998; Abraham and Kumar, 1999).

One of the studies pointed out that adolescents need help to acquire socially appropriate sexual behaviour, to make safe sexual choices, and to become less vulnerable to sexual abuse (McCabe, 1996).

Many of the studies have shown that adolescents had poor knowledge of sexually Transmitted Infections (STIs) (Awasthi and Pande, 1998; Dash, 2004; Sahoo, 2004; NACO, MOHFW, and GOI, 2005; McManus and Dhar, 2008). Sexually Transmitted Infections are high among male because they practiced unsafe sex and among girls because of their biological susceptibility and ignorance (Sharma and Sharma, 1997, Abraham, 1998). Various myths prevail related to STIs such as, STIs caused by having sexual intercourse with a woman during her menstrual period, STIs could be cured by having sex with a virgin (Sharma and Sharma, 1997).

Most adolescents have heard about HIV/AIDS but few know enough to protect them against infections. (Aggarwal and Kumar, 1997; Basin *et al.*,1997; Sundar *et al.*, 1997). Several misconceptions persist about mode of transmission (Amalraj *et al.*, 1997; Khan and Singh, 1997; Rahate *et al.*, 1997; Sahoo, 2004).

A study indicated that adolescents who smoked or consumed alcohol were likely to be indulged in unprotected sexual intercourse before marriage and highly susceptible to the contraction and transmission of HIV/AIDS and other sexually Transmitted Infections (Awasthi and Pande, 1998).

Sources of Information Accessed by the Adolescent Students about Reproductive Health Issues

Adolescents are considered sexually mature, but reproductive health issues are rarely discussed with unmarried adolescents. In fact, reproductive health issues are not even discussed openly in the family or society. Many of the studies reviewed in this section would explore the sources of information accessed by the adolescents on reproductive health issues. In this section sixteen studies were reviewed.

Ahuja and Tiwari (1995) found in the their study that in the school-going girls, friends followed by the mothers were the major source of information regarding reproductive health matters, whereas in the non-school-going girls, it was mainly mothers followed by older sisters or sisters-in-law.

Khan *et al.,* (1996) provided an analysis of exposure to various mass media. The findings showed little difference between the male and female students, except in the case of newspapers. More boys (74%) than girls (57%) read them daily. A comparison between types of schools (government and private), revealed a significant difference in the choice of media. Students in private schools depended more on print media, whereas the public school students favoured the radio. T.V. was used equally by both groups. Television, books, and magazines were the main sources of contraceptive information. Friends were another important source.

Bahulekar and Garg (1997) has stated that seven per cent adolescents in their study had received information through health personnel.

Lal *et al.,* (1997) revealed that adolescent students were unanimously aware of AIDS. Newspapers (67.4%), followed by T.V. (49.4%), magazines (41.6%), friends (30.4%), and radio (23.6%), were cited as the most common sources of information by the students, irrespective of the location of their college, subject of study, and gender. All the sources above were significantly more popular with urban' students, except for friends, a source significantly more popular among rural students.

Awasthi and Pande (1998) revealed that the primary sources of knowledge about sex were friends, television, magazines and books, and siblings. The immediate initiation of reproductive health counseling programmes is recommended

It was found by Sachdev (1998) that basic knowledge regarding sexual anatomy and function was inadequate among both males and females, and this knowledge was obtained primarily from friends and books and rarely from parents.

Thapa and Rawal (1998) studied the sources of information regarding sex were friends, T.V., cinema, books, and the Internet. The data revealed the need to incorporate sex education in the school curriculum.

A study conducted by Singh, Devi and Gupta (1999) reported that for almost all the adolescent girls aged 13-17 in Haryana, the leading source of information was television (73%) and/or radio (37%).

Bhatia and Swami (2000) expressed concern about the low levels of knowledge in the rural girls regarding fertility control methods particularly, because three fourths of the country's populations stay in villages. The crucial role that schools, parents, students, and social organizations can play in strengthening adolescent reproductive health programmes is discussed.

Thakor and Kumar (2000) in their study stated that doctors and teachers were preferred as the source for imparting sex education, doctors still remained the first choice for imparting sex education.

Abraham (2001) in her study reflected that among low-income college boys in Mumbai, erotic materials were the main source of information. Television, peers and erotic literature are the most commonly cited sources of information on sexual and reproductive matters although the information they provide is not always accurate.

NACO and UNICEF (2002) in a National Behavioural Surveillance Survey suggested that by and large, young people are relatively unexposed to the large range of media providing messages on HIV/AIDS: while 76 per cent were exposed to such messages on television, far fewer (between one-third and half) were exposed to messages through the radio or newspapers/ magazines, and between 6 per cent and 12 per cent through billboards, pamphlets or films. In contrast, even fewer about 15 per cent of males and females were exposed to inter-personal communication on the topic.

Dash (2004), found in his study titled "reproductive health problems of unmarried adolescent girls" that girls consulted their mothers mainly on reproductive health problems.

In the study conducted by Sahoo (2004), adolescents pointed out that parents and guardians were main obstacles to gain knowledge on reproductive and sexual health. It was recommended by the study that it is necessary to make parents aware of these issues. Parent teacher association should be effectively involved. Teacher should be selected as friendly adviser and train them. Question box can be set up in each school, IEC material be developed and collected and distributed.

Acharya and Dasgupta (2005) adopted a right based approach; the study explores widely the needs of adolescents in general and those of sexuality in particular. An in-depth analysis of contemporary and relevant policies has been undertaken in context of adolescents. A small field study of Jaunsari Tribes of Uttranchal has been incorporated to demonstrate the key issues. In-depth interview, FGDs with unmarried females and males in age group 15-19 were conducted. The results reflected that there is absence of a source to satisfy the queries on health and sexual matters, including HIV/AIDS, contraceptives and menstruation related problems.Young adults' sites that they know about HIV/AIDS but are not clear as to the causes etc. Pointed out that advertisements in Doordarshan and Radio do not clearly explain the causes and how and why does it happen. All information they get from peers and video films that they watch in village. It was reported by the respondents that In village Kalsi Johdi—A young PHC worker usually available and helped them and answered their queries and girls usually get information from mother, elder sisters and sister-in-law.

Findings of the study conducted by Prasad (2006) to study the perception on Sexual Matters Among Rural Adolescent Boys represents that more than one-fifth of adolescent boys (22%) were inclined to read sex related issues published in periodicals than half of the adolescents (50%) who used to read a little. Half of the adolescent boys (50%) had read letters to editor on sex issues. Two-fifth of teenage boys (40%) opined that sex related articles were useful to unmarried boys. They believed that articles published in magazines were useful and should be made available to unmarried boys. Forty eight per cent acquired knowledge on sex indirectly through observation, whereas Thirty nine per cent assimilated sex knowledge directly through discussion with peers group or relatives.

Above Reviewed studies suggest that friends were most preferable source of information for the adolescents on reproductive health issues (Khan et al., 1996; Acharya and Dasgupta, 2005; Sachdev, 1998; Thapa and Rawal, 1998). Researchers reflected that teachers and doctors were also preferred as the source for imparting reproductive health education (Thakor and Kumar, 2000; Sahoo, 2004; Bahulekar and Garg, 1997). Mothers were major source of information for girls (Dash, 2004). Studies revealed that primary source of information on reproductive health issues were T.V./Radio, books, magazine, and siblings (Acharya and Dasgupta, 2005; Thapa and Rawal, 1998; Lal et al., 1997; Awasthi and pande, 1998). It can be seen that television, peers and erotic literature are the most commonly cited sources of information on sexual and reproductive matters although the information they provide some times not accurate (Abraham, 2001; Acharya and Dasgupta, 2005).

Opinion of Parents towards Reproductive Health Education for Adolescents

Reproductive health issues are taboo subjects within families. In many cases, parents believe that talking to adolescents about these matters would imply approval of sexual activity. Concern for the sexual security and chastity of daughters appears to dominate parental relationships with adolescent girls. While parents closely supervise the activities of adolescent daughters in an attempt to inhibit sexual activity, they often condone the sexual activity of their sons. However, relationships in which parents take on a policing role may not always safeguard against risky sexual behaviour: intimate non-sexual and even sexual relations does indeed occur, and unwanted pregnancy and resort to abortion are not unknown, notwithstanding parental perceptions (Mehra, Savithri and Coutinho, 2002). In this section four studies were reviewed:

Study Conducted by Abraham and Kumar (1999) on low-income college students in Mumbai reveals a positive relationship between perceived authoritarian family relationships and early sexual debut among young males

Another study of 16-year-old students in Goa suggests that adolescents

— especially girls, who experience unwanted sexual relations, are more likely than others to report lack of communication and support in the relationship with their parents (Patel and Andrew, 2001).

Ganatra and Hirve (2002) found that adolescent abortion-seekers suggests that fear of parents, fear of disclosure of pregnancy status and lack of perceived parental support may have led many pregnant adolescents to delay an abortion or to seek an abortion from unqualified providers.

Masilamani (2003) in the study titled "Building a supportive environment for adolescent reproductive health programmes: Essential programme components " stressed on the fact that parents increasingly recognize the importance of raising awareness among their adolescent children but are inhibited by lack of in-depth knowledge and embarrassment to do this themselves.

Studies have indicated that lack of communication and support exists in the relationship between adolescents and their parents (Abraham and Kumar, 1999; Patel and Andrew, 2001). Adolescent females who, experienced unwanted sexual relations have a fear of disclosure of pregnancy status. Lack of perceived parental support may have led many pregnant adolescents to delay an abortion or to seek an abortion from unqualified providers (Patel and Andrew, 2001; Ganatra and Hirve, 2002). Most parents felt inadequate to talk to their children about issues related to reproductive health (Abraham and Kumar, 1999; Masilamani, 2003).

Opinion of Teachers about Need of Imparting Reproductive Health Education to Adolescents

Reproductive Health Education in School is nowadays an important public health issue as it concerns not only adolescent pregnancy prevention and AIDS prevention and other sexually transmitted infections but also interpersonal relationships and psychosocial issues. Therefore reproductive health education in school contributes to promote better citizenship. Sexuality presents a multidimensional aspect and concern deeply humans in the interweaving between sexuality, social influences, cognitive and affective development. So sexuality can be reduce in a dichotomy biology/psychology and involve in same time psycho-affective and biological maturation and social learning (WHO, 1999; WHO, 2006). These conceptions have an impact on practices. Teachers seem reticent to implement Reproductive Health Education especially the social aspects (relationship, emotions, affects, equality, gender issues, sex orientation…). Two studies were reviewed in this section:

Study conducted by Verma and Pauri (1997) carried out with selected students and teachers from 18 randomly chosen schools of rural Maharashtra. Focus group discussions were conducted on AIDS, sex and sexuality, sex education, and role of teachers in providing AIDS related information. Male and female teachers participated together in the discussion, whereas separate student groups were formed for boys and girls. Results showed unawareness of AIDS among most of the students. Most of the teachers showed unwillingness to discuss sex-related topics with the students.

Bhasin and Aggarwal (1999) in their study brought the attention towards the need for creating awareness regarding responsible reproductive behaviour among adolescents, due to the rising incidence of HIV/AIDS among the youth and prevailing trends in Indian society that consider sex to be a tabooed subject. The cross-sectional study conducted by Bhasin and Aggarwal (1999) aimed at finding out the perceptions of senior secondary school teachers (N=476) regarding imparting of sex education to children. Their perceptions were considered important to facilitate learning regarding reproductive behaviour among adolescents. A majority of the teachers were in favour of imparting sex education. Possible content included reproductive anatomy and physiology, family planning, sexually transmitted diseases, dating, premarital sex, and sexual perversions. Those who opposed sex education cited reasons such as irrelevance of topic, not in accordance with the culture, increased promiscuity, and sex related crimes. The most appropriate age for commencing sex education was considered to be 14 years and ninth class. Teachers were willing to impart sex education after receiving proper training. Biology teachers were considered to be the most appropriate subject teachers, followed by doctors.

Researchers have discussed that the teachers' perceptions considered important to impart reproductive health education among adolescents. A majority of the teachers were in favour of imparting sex education (Bhasin and Aggarwal, 1999). In another study Most of the teachers showed unwillingness to discuss sex-related topics with the students (Verma and Pauri, 1997). Those who opposed sex education cited reasons such as irrelevance of topic, not in accordance with the culture, increased promiscuity, and sex related crimes. Teachers were willing to impart sex education after receiving proper training (Bhasin and Aggarwal, 1999).

Interventions/ Recommendations in Order to Impart Appropriate Knowledge and Attitude among Adolescents Regarding Reproductive Health Issues

Adolescents are considered to be vulnerable to reproductive health problems, and there is a need for developing healthy attitudes through reproductive health education. In this section eleven studies were reviewed.

The researchers Ahuja and Tiwari (1995) recommended the introduction of family life education from class VII onwards, and educating mothers as well as male members of the families of non-school-going adolescent girls from rural communities.

The study conducted by Bhende (1995) covers the following aspects: knowledge regarding menstruation, physical changes during puberty, reproduction, sexual aspects of marriage, and STDs and HIV/AIDS; opinions, perceptions, and values regarding love marriages, future partner, "bad girl/ boy", and restrictions on girls; and sexual behaviour including social interaction between adolescent girls and boys, reaction to sexual harassment, and premarital sexual behaviour. One point that clearly emerged from the various sources of data was that adolescent girls were vigilantly protected, their movements were strictly restricted, and non-compliance was severely dealt with. These girls were not sexually active, and friendly interaction with boys was superficial and mainly non-verbal communication. Research findings indicated that the girls utterly lacked power-power that stems from knowledge about their bodies and bodily functions, power of decision making, power to break away from the "culture of silence" they are forced into, resulting in poor self-image and self-esteem. Hence the study stressed on developing educational intervention for the girls not only concentrate on the sexual aspects, but cover themes relevant to their lives, themes that built up their confidence and self-esteem to deal with current and future problems. Indirect evidence showed boys at a different stage of sexual development, emphasizing the need for a different approach.

In a study by Jejeebhoy (1996) several programme and research recommendations stand out and are briefly elaborated upon. The programme recommendations are: (1) intensify efforts to postpone early marriage; (2) address the negative health implications of the lack of autonomy of married adolescent girls; (3) fulfill the nutritional needs of adolescent girls; (4) provide more education to adolescents on anatomy and physiology; and (5) respond more sensitively to special needs of unmarried adolescent girls and boys.

The role that youth, anganwadi and social workers, and women's groups can play in ensuring the implementation of recommendations is elaborated in the study carried out by Atwood and Hussein (1997). Delaying early marriages, preventing conception, birth spacing, long-term support, and adequate mention at the policy level are considered to be crucial steps towards prevention of adolescent pregnancy. For adolescents who have already become mothers, the need to provide them and their newborns with accessible and appropriate care is suggested. Atwood and Hussein (1997).

Bahulekar and Garg (1997) strongly emphasized on the need for intensive AIDS educational programmes through schools, mass media, health workers, and community leaders.

Abraham (1998) has revealed that Sex education programmes did not reach the college youth despite government efforts. Recommendations include curriculum integration, a congenial educational environment, and student involvement in sex education programmes.

The study by Thakor and Kumar (2000) assessed the impact of sex education amongst adolescents (need perception, knowledge and attitude regarding reproductive health issues), evaluated feasibility and acceptance of the programme, and suggested a model for providing quality sex education. The lectures dealt with anatomy and physiology of the reproductive system and cleared up misconceptions regarding sexual behaviour. The study recommended that knowledge regarding sex education, appreciation of the role of contraceptives (more for boys), willingness to participate in sex education for girls, and added knowledge regarding conception needs to be improved.

Study conducted by Kirby (2001) reflected that the early access to information is the best way not only to prevent sexual violence and sexual transmitted infections but also to promote sexual health and more largely health education. School-based sexuality education is an important and effective way of enhancing young people's knowledge, attitudes and behaviour. There is widespread agreement that formal education should include sexuality education.

In a study carried out by Yadav (2003) it was highlighted that a large majority of adolescent students desired that reproductive health education should be given in schools. Though their responses varied regarding how and who should do it, whether parents or school or both, whether through integration or as a separate subject or through co-curricular activities or a combination of all, however, majority desired that both school and parents should help them clarify adolescents reproductive health related issues.

Dash (2004) in his study recommended (1) Life skill education on self assertiveness, self confidence and negotiation skills should be developed (2) Fly life education including sexuality education provide as a part of school curriculum (3) Capacity building of adolescent girls needs to be initiated by training and sensitization.

Study conducted by Berger (2005) stressed that effective school programmes would include the following elements: (1) A focus on scientific information about human reproduction, providing accurate information about contraception and birth control; (2) A basis in theories which explain what influences people's sexual choices and behaviour and gender issue (3) A clear, and continuously reinforced message about sexual behaviour and risk reduction; (4) Working on psychosocial abilities, self esteem, dealing with peer and other social pressures on young people; providing opportunities to practise communication, negotiation and assertion skills; (5) Uses a variety of approaches to teaching and learning that involve and engage young people and help them to personalise the information; (6) Uses approaches to teaching and learning which are appropriate to young people's age, experience and cultural background. Formal programmes with these elements have been shown to increase young people's levels of knowledge about sex and sexuality, decrease risk when they do have sex. All the elements are important and interrelated, and sexuality education needs to be supported by links to sexual health services, otherwise it is not going to be so effective. It also takes into account the messages about sexual values and behaviour young people get from other sources, like friends and the media. It is also responsive to the needs of the young people themselves - whether they are girls or boys, on their own or in a single sex or mixed sex group, and what they know already, their age and experiences.

Studies reflected that school-based reproductive health education is an important and effective way of enhancing young people's knowledge, attitudes and behaviour (Abraham, 1998; Kirby 2001). Though opinions varied regarding how and who should do it, whether parents or school or both, whether through integration or as a separate subject or through co-curricular activities or a combination of all, however, majority desired that both school and parents should help them clarify adolescents reproductive health related issues. It was recommended by the researches that it should be given from class VI onwards and both male and female members of the family needs to be educated on reproductive health issues of the adolescents (Yadav, 2003; Ahuja and Tiwari, 1995). Aspects to be covered suggested by the various researchers were: knowledge regarding menstruation, physical changes during puberty, reproduction, contraception and birth control; and STIs and HIV/AIDS and sexual behaviour including social interaction between adolescent girls and boys, reaction to sexual harassment, and premarital sexual behaviour. Life skill education on self assertiveness, self confidence and negotiation skills should be developed. Capacity building of adolescents need to be initiated by training and sensitization (Bhende, 1995; Jejeebhoy, 1996; Atwood and Hussein, 1997; Thakor and Kumar, 2000; Dash, 2004; Berger, 2005).

Overview of Literature Appraised

Majority of studies were descriptive in nature, where researchers were found to be interested to describe the awareness level of adolescents on reproductive health issues including HIV/AIDS. In the reviewed studies, parents' opinion on imparting reproductive health education was not studied, while two studies assessed the teachers' perception on providing reproductive health education. Not even a single study covered all the reproductive health issues together (holistic), previous research studies concentrated on one or two issues of reproductive health like —

- Adolescents' sexuality and sexual behaviour (Mehra, Savithri, and Coutinho, 2002); Sharma and Sharma, 1997; Jejeebhoy, 2000; Awasthi and Pande, 1998; Bhende, 1995).
- Awareness on reproductive health issues/Awareness of AIDS among school children/ awareness regarding pubertal changes (Yadav, 2003;

Verma and Pauri, 1997, Tikoo *et al.*, 1997, Sundar *et al.*, 1997; Sharma and Sharma, 1996; Rahate, *et al.,* 1997; Shilpa and Ratnakumari, 1999; Sahoo, 2004; Sachdev, 1998; Ahuja and Tewari, 1995).

- Reproductive health problems of unmarried adolescent girls (Dash, 2004, and Harms *et al.*, 1998).
- Fertility control methods: Knowledge of adolescents (Gupta and Khan, 1996; Bhatia and Swami, 2000).

Issues related to substance abuse and sexual abuse have a strong relation with reproductive health but it is not been covered properly by the researches in the field of reproductive health. Substance abuse covered by the study on sexual behaviour patterns and knowledge of sexually transmitted diseases in adolescent boys (Awasthi and Pande, 1998). Issue related to Sexual abuse was covered by the study on sex education programmes for people with mental retardation (McCabe, 1996).

However number of studies did not mention their research design, but while addressing this issue researcher's limited access to journals and literature available online can not be ignored.

Review indicates that most of the studies were exclusively undertaken with girls, some of the studies with the boys, and very few of the studies done with both boys and girls together.

Review of studies also indicates that a large number of studies have used quantitative techniques for data collection, very few studies used qualitative techniques and three used both quantitative and qualitative techniques.

Most of the studies used questionnaire or standardized inventories as a tool for data collection because of the time constraint involved with the school students and this also suggests that the tools, which can collect data in short span of time and do not require long term interaction with respondents may be best suited for research in this field.

Most of the studies used probability sampling methods to draw the required sample where mainly simple random and systematic sampling was used.

The research studies conducted on reproductive health have rarely considered it important to include unmarried adolescents in their sample. In India, reproductive health was studied traditionally as part of demographic studies in relation to family planning with in marriage. In recent years, it has become part of the HIV/AIDS research into sex related risk behaviour (Amalraj *et al.,* 1997; Acharya and Dasgupta, 2005; Goyal, 1995; and Bhasin *et al.,* 1997) Research into reproductive health from the perspective of family planning focuses mainly on married couples and AIDS research focuses on specific groups-at-risk. Both kinds of research tend to leave out the adolescent group. The review suggests that there is a need to investigate on awareness and attitude towards reproductive health issues among more representative samples of adolescent boys and girls.

As indicated by many studies that most of the adolescents have little knowledge of reproductive and sexual health (Sahoo, 2004; Chaudhary, 1998; Yadav, 2003). Lack of knowledge regarding human reproduction has caused some young people to engage in risky sexual behaviour. Literature review has shown that adolescents are becoming sexually active at a younger age. The age of which sexual activity begins varies from 12-18 years (Abraham, 1998; Awasthi and Pande, 1998; Acharya and Das gupta 2005; Sharma and Sharma, 1995). The trends indicate greater permissiveness towards premarital sex (Awasthi and Pande, 1998 and, Sharma and Sharma, 1995) Adolescent have misconception, myths and little access to correct information and knowledge about sex, sexuality and reproductive health (Ahuja and Tewari, 1995; Awasthi and Pande, 1998; Bhasin *et al.,* 1997; and, Acharya and Das Gupta, 2005) Studies have shown that misconception existed, more among females than males (Amalraj *et al.,* 1997; Abraham, 1998; Shilpa and Ratna Kumari, 1999) Most of the studies have recommended the need for comprehensive reproductive health education (Awasthi and Pande, 1998; Abraham, 1998; Ahuja and Tewari, 1995; Shilpa and Ratnakumari, 1999). Studies also discussed the crucial role that schools and parents can play in strengthening adolescent reproductive health programme (Bhatia and Swami, 2000; Acharya and Dasgupta, 2005). Studies have stressed that adolescent sexuality should be geared in a positive way for boy and girls (Bhasin and Aggarwal, 1999; and Acharya and Dasgupta, 2005) and the concept of sexual behaviours can also be clarified and inculcated during this phase of life.

The studies carried out so far on reproductive health issues have identified a number of pathways through which different factors may influence reproductive health of adolescents. Although there are several empirical studies focusing on level of knowledge of adolescents and youth on one or other component of reproductive health but no comprehensive study including all the components of reproductive health have been conducted. Thus the author proposed a study that includes all the components related to adolescents' reproductive health.

Review further suggests that comparatively much empirical evidence exist on studying adolescents' knowledge, attitude and perception, but there are few studies have been conducted to understand the perspective of both adolescents and teachers on imparting reproductive health education in schools (Bhasin and Aggarwal, 1999; Sharma and Sharma, 1995). Review reflects that almost all the studies recommended the involvement of parents in imparting reproductive health education amongst adolescents but no empirical evidences found where the parents' opinion and concerns regarding their adolescents' reproductive health issues and education have been studied. Thus, the present research is holistic in nature, including adolescents, school teachers as well parents in order to study various dimensions related to reproductive health education for adolescents.

The limited research and mixed results concerning influence of various factors on reproductive health dictate the need for additional research exclusively on adolescents reproductive Health. The present research attempted to address some of the issues that still needs to examine like, identification of the reproductive health needs of adolescents by using both qualitative and quantitative techniques so that findings can have a strong base for drawing rationale and explanations, documentation and evaluation of existing adolescents' programmes, designing various approaches to address reproductive health needs of adolescents, and also ensuring involvement of parents, teachers and at large community also.

3

National Policies and Programmes: A Brief Analysis

Adolescents constitute significant proportion of any population by several criteria, such as size, amount of energy and enthusiasm, the number of productive years at their hands to contribute to the human and material resources, to the social and political life of the country. Owing to its untouched resource potentials, adolescents form the future hope of that nation as well. Policies and programmes have a profound impact on healthy development of adolescents. However, until recently, policies and programmes in India have focused very little on the adolescent group. Over the past 50 years, the population has grown at a rapid pace and so, too, has the adolescent population, despite a formal and a well-organized family planning programme in India. Until quite recently, the approach of the family planning programme has focused on achieving demographic goals by increasing use of contraceptives. The commitment of the national government to the reproductive health approach forged at the International Conference on Population and Development (ICPD) in 1994 has reshaped the family welfare programme into a broad-based Reproductive and Child Health (RCH) Services Programme in India. Policymakers and planners have now realized that the adolescents have specific health and developmental needs. There is a growing understanding that adolescence is a bridge between childhood and adulthood. The newer focus on RCH also has been invigorated by the continuing realization of the importance of women's health. It is now well accepted that if the health of women is to be improved, the health of adolescents must be given high priority in Indian policy, programme development and implementation.

Keeping in mind that adolescence is a transition phase through which a child becomes an adult. It is also the period during which rapid physical growth, physiological and psychosocial changes, the development of secondary sexual characteristics, and reproductive maturation occur. During adolescence, an intense sexual drive develops and adolescents typically start exploring relationships with the opposite sex. Adolescents start defining social relationships outside the family. Their behaviour is guided by an intense desire for independence and identity. In the process, adolescents undergo intense psychological stress and personality change (Rao, 1995). India has articulated its commitment to promote and protect the reproductive and sexual rights of adolescents through its policies and in several forums.

Adolescent reproductive health rights and needs were placed on the international agenda for the first time by the International Conference on Population and Development (ICPD), Cairo, 1994. The Cairo Plan of Action recognized the specific sexual and reproductive health needs of adolescents beyond the "disease" and "procreation" dimensions and focused on the overall health, Sexual and Reproductive health (SRH) rights, and well-being of adolescents.

ICPD RECOGNIZED ADOLESCENTS' RIGHTS TO REPRODUCTIVE HEALTH

"...Countries must ensure that the programmes and attitudes of health-care providers do not restrict the access of adolescents to appropriate services and the information they need...these services must safeguard the rights of adolescents to privacy, confidentiality, respect and informed consent, respecting cultural values and religious beliefs." (Para. 7.45)

"Countries, with the support of the international community, should protect and promote the rights of adolescents to reproductive health education, information and care and greatly reduce the number of adolescent pregnancies." (Para. 7.46)

"...Programmes should include support mechanisms for the education and counselling of adolescents in the areas of gender relations and equality, violence against adolescents, responsible sexual behaviour, responsible family-planning practice, family life, reproductive health, sexually transmitted diseases, HIV infection and AIDS prevention... Adolescents must be fully involved in the planning, implementation and evaluation." (Para.7.47)

"Programmes should involve and train all who are in a position to provide guidance to adolescents concerning responsible sexual and reproductive behaviour, particularly parents and families, and also communities, religious institutions, schools, the mass media and peer groups." (Para. 7.48)

(United Nations, 1994)

Millennium Development Goal (MDG) Interventions by Area as Recommended by the UN Millennium Project

Governments from all over the world met at the 2005 World Summit to reaffirm their resolve to achieve the Millennium Development Goals by 2015. Many of the MDG targets directly relate to adolescents' health and development. Social investments in adolescent's education, health, and employment can enable countries to build a strong economic base, thereby reversing intergenerational poverty. Such investments, if timely and gender equal can help countries to achieve other MDGs such as universalizing education, promoting gender equality, reducing maternal mortality, and reversing the rising tide of HIV in young people. The World Summit underscored the need for achieving universal access to reproductive health services by 2015, as set out in the ICPD.

Reproductive health intervention recommended by the UN Millennium Project (2005) is presented below:

INTERVENTION AREA 1: INVESTMENT IN RURAL DEVELOPMENT

Investments in rural development include interventions in poverty and hunger reduction; domestic water supply, sanitation, and water management infrastructure; rural transport; and rural energy services.

Nutrition

Nutrition for infants, pregnant women, and nursing mothers

Promotion of mother- and baby-friendly community initiatives, including exclusive breastfeeding for first 6 months and complementary feeding with continuing breastfeeding for infants ages 7–24 months. HIV-positive mothers should use replacement feeding when it is acceptable, feasible, affordable, sustainable, and safe. Provision of sufficient calories, protein, and micronutrients to pregnant women and nursing mothers, supported by nutrition extension workers and using locally produced food to the extent possible.

Intervention Area 3: Investments in the Health System

Investments in the health system include interventions in child and maternal health; prevention, care, and treatment of HIV/AIDS, TB, and malaria; access to essential medicines; measures to strengthen health systems management and health services delivery; and sexual and reproductive health.

Child Health

Neonatal integrated package

It includes Clean delivery, newborn resuscitation, prevention of hypothermia, kangaroo care (skin-to-skin contact), antibiotics for infection, tetanus toxoid (TT), breastfeeding education (including education on replacement feeding for HIV-positive mothers) and hygiene education.

Integrated Management of Childhood Illness plus Immunization

Integrated approach to reduce child mortality, illness, and disability, includes both preventive and curative elements to address leading causes of child mortality such as oral rehydration therapy and antibiotics for diarrheal disease, antibiotics for acute respiratory infection, care for measles, anti-malarials for malaria, and nutritional supplements for malnutrition plus immunization.

Maternal Health

Emergency Obstetric Care

It contains rapidly accessible treatment for delivery complications such as eclampsia, hemorrhage, obstructed labour, and sepsis. Emergency obstetric care requires functioning referral systems and well equipped and staffed district hospitals.

(*Contd.*)

Skilled Attendance, Clean Delivery, and Post-partum Care

Presence of trained and registered midwives, nurses, nurse-midwives, or doctors at birth with ability to diagnose and refer emergent complications as well as post-partum care (including counseling on nutrition, family planning, and parenthood skills).

Antenatal care

Routine care during pregnancy, including preventive and curative interventions such as blood pressure and weight monitoring, treatment of infections, nutrition and smoking counseling, intermittent preventive treatment for malaria, and anti-retrovirals for HIV-positive women to prevent mother-to-child transmission of HIV.

Safe Abortion Services

Access to post-abortion care, access to abortion counseling and, where permitted by law, safe abortion services.

HIV/AIDS Prevention

Improved linkages

Effective joint programming between reproductive health and HIV/AIDS programmes.

Behaviour Change Programmes

Programmes to encourage safer sexual behaviour, including condom social marketing, peer-based education, mass media campaigns, work-based programmes, and school-based HIV education.

Control of Sexually Transmitted Diseases

Routine screening and effective treatment of sexually transmitted diseases (such as syphilis, gonorrhea, and chlamydia).

Voluntary Counseling and Testing

Pre- and post-test counseling and HIV testing.

Harm Reduction for Injecting Drug Users

Actions to prevent transmission of HIV and other infections that occur through sharing of non-sterile injection equipment and drug preparations; specific programmes include provision of sterile syringes and needles and drug substitution treatment.

Prevention of Mother-to-child Transmission

Prevention of transmission of HIV from infected women to their infants during pregnancy, labour, and delivery, as well as during breastfeeding (that is, replacement feeding when it is acceptable, feasible, affordable, sustain-able, and safe); includes short-term antiretroviral prophylactic treatment; infant feeding, counseling, and support; and the use of safer infant feeding methods.

Blood Safety Interventions

Measures to reduce the risk of receiving infected blood through a transfusion, including HIV antibody screening, protocols to avoid unnecessary blood transfusions, and policies to exclude high-risk donors.

HIV/AIDS Care and Treatment

Antiretroviral therapy

(Contd.)

Combination Drug Therapy to Treat AIDS.

Treatment of Opportunistic Infections

Treatment of any infection caused by a microorganism that would not normally cause disease in a healthy individual.

Orphan Support

Provision of support to orphans to minimize the impact of AIDS on their lives; includes school fee support, community support, and support to extended families.

Access to Essential Medicine

Interventions to ensure availability, affordability, and appropriate use

Incentives to direct research and development processes toward appropriate med-icines for developing countries; establishment of national essential medicines lists (including preventive, curative, and reproductive health commodities, equipment, and supplies); ensuring reliable procurement and distribution systems; prequalifying quality suppliers and procurement and distribution facilities; monitoring systems to assure drug quality; elimination of user fees for essential medicines; programmes to improve the way drugs are prescribed, dispensed, and used, including public media campaigns and education of providers.

Health Systems

Multiple interventions to strengthen health system

Human resource training and salary enhancement, improving management capacity, enhancing monitoring and evaluation, strengthening quality control, strengthening medical information systems, increasing capacity for research and development, enhancing community demand, and improving infrastructure.

Sexual and Reproductive Health

(Elements of integrated programming not covered under maternal health, child health, HIV/AIDS programmes)

Counseling on Contraception and Birth Spacing

Information and education on benefits and methods of family planning and birth spacing, appropriate follow-up on method satisfaction, consistent and correct use of method, and options for appropriate method switching.

Universal access to Contraception

Programme to ensure universal access to family planning choices, including effective modern contraceptive methods, and to guarantee reliably available and affordable supplies and choice among methods.

Age-appropriate Sexuality Education and Services *(Especially for Adolescents)*

School and community-based education programmes, mass media education programmes, youth-friendly information and service delivery, beneficiary-driven programming to meet the information and service needs of diverse adolescent groups (including married adolescents), and programmes to educate parents to improve adolescent reproductive health.

Prevention and Treatment of Sexually Transmitted Infections (STIs)

Programmes to detect and treat STIs (such as syphilis, gonorrhea, and chlamydia) and other reproductive tract infections that can increase the risk of HIV/AIDS and infertility and affect the choice of appropriate contraceptive methods.

Outreach to Men to Increase Participation and Support in Reproductive Health

Counseling and information services for men to address their reproductive health

(*Contd.*)

needs, support the decisions of their partners, and change gender and relationship norms to ensure greater gender equality; prevent gender violence and harmful traditional practices and promote collaborative decision-making; information and services for reproductive health in the army and police forces, including efforts to combat gender violence.

Intervention Area 5: Investments in Gender Equality

Investments in gender equality include interventions for sexual and reproductive health access to property rights and work, security, participation and institutional reform, and data collection and monitoring.

Sexual and Reproductive Health (SRH)

Universal access to SRH information and services and protection of reproductive rights (Service packages described under health interventions above).

Legislation and awareness campaigns to protect the rights of individuals and couples to plan their families; to ensure access to sexual and reproductive health information and services; to discourage early marriage (at ages posing health risks), female genital mutilation, and other traditional harmful practices; and to expand access to safe abortions (where permitted by law) and review the legal status of abortion in order to improve public health while respecting national sovereignty, cultural values, and diversity.

Security

Security for girls and women from violence

Legislation and administrative actions to protect women against violence, promotion of awareness of women's right to seek redress, protection from perpetrators of violence (through access to shelters, services, and so on) and mechanisms to dispense justice to perpetrators.

Source: UN Millennium Project, 2005.

India has endorsed the International Conference on Population and Development (ICPD), and the ICPD+5 Programme of Action, and made a commitment to, "protect and promote the right of adolescents to the enjoyment of the highest attainable standard of health" (IISD, 1999). India was one of the first countries to ratify, in 1992, the Convention on the Rights of the Child. India has also signed the Convention on the Elimination of All Forms of Discrimination against Women that reinforces the rights of adolescent females. It is also evident that the realization and sustainability of the Millennium Development Goals rests, to a considerable extent, on the reproductive and sexual health situation of adolescents.

In this chapter, the author focused on the national policies and vision documents pertaining to population, youth, health, HIV/AIDS prevention and control, women's empowerment and education. The policy documents studied are the National Youth Policy 2003, the National Health Policy 2002, the National AIDS Prevention and Control Policy 2002, the National Policy for the Empowerment of Women 2001, the National Population Policy 2000 and the National Policy on Education 1986 (as modified in 1992).

The author also pay the attention towards the national programme documents, including national and state programme Implementation Plans (PIPs) of the RCH Programme II, National AIDS Control Programme (NACP)-III, National Population Education Programme (NPEP), School AIDS education programme, YUVA School Adolescents Education Programme (SAEP) SCERT and the annual reports of various ministries, including Health and Family Welfare, Youth Affairs and Sports, Human Resource Development, Women and Child Development and AIDS Control Organisation.

National Policies related to Reproductive Health of the Adolescents

Various Ministries of the government of India have developed policies related to Adolescents Reproductive Health. A number of policies reaffirming a commitment to young people were formulated in the 1970s and 1980s, including the National Policy for Children 1974 and the National Youth Policy 1985. However, these initiatives paid only superficial attention to the health needs and concerns of adolescents. The significant shift in the way population and reproductive health problems were conceptualised during the 1990s brought about greater attention to the health concerns of adolescents. This attention is clearly reflected in several policies adopted since the 1990s. Notable among national policies that address adolescents' sexual and reproductive health needs and rights are:

- National Population Policy, 2000
- National AIDS Prevention and Control Policy 2002
- National Youth Policy, 2003
- National Policy on Education 1986 (Modified 1992)
- National Policy for the Empowerment of Women 2001 (MOWCD 2001)
- National Health Policy, 2002
- Tenth and Eleventh Five Year Plans
- National Adolescent Reproductive and Sexual Health Strategy

The National Population Policy 2000

The National Population Policy 2000 recognized, for the first time, that adolescents constitute an under-served group with special sexual and reproductive health needs, and advocates special programmatic attention to addressing this population. It recommends the need to ensure for adolescents access to sexual and reproductive health information, and counselling and services that are affordable and accessible. It also underscores the need to "strengthen primary health centres and sub-centres to provide counselling, both to adolescents and also to newly-weds". The Policy also advocates special programmatic attention to delay age at marriage and to enforce the Child Marriage Restraint Act 1976. The major thrust to adolescent health, however, was given in the National Population Policy 2000. Recognizing that the needs of adolescents, including the need for protection from unwanted pregnancies and STIs, have not been specifically addressed in the past, India's National Population Policy 2000 underscored adolescent health as a strategic focus in achieving socio-demographic goals. The policy aims at ensuring that adolescents' need for information, counseling, population education, and contraceptive services are accessible and affordable; food supplements and nutrition services are available; and the legislation on restraint of child marriage is enforced. The population policy also emphasized that reproductive health services for adolescent girls and boys are especially needed in rural areas, where adolescent marriage and pregnancy are most prevalent. The policy also underscored the need for programmes that encourage delayed marriage and childbearing and the need for education about the risks of unprotected sex (Government of India, 2000).

National AIDS Prevention and Control Policy 2002

The growth of the HIV/AIDS epidemic in India and the recognition of its spread among young people have resulted in a greater openness in addressing issues relating to sex among young people. Recognising the special vulnerability of youth, the National AIDS Prevention and Control Policy 2002 notes the need to promote a better understanding of HIV infection and safer sex practices among youth. The objective of the Policy is to spread information among "students, youth and other sexually active sections to generate greater awareness about the nature of its transmission and to adopt safe behavioural practices for prevention" through programmes especially designed to meet their needs. The Policy stresses a variety of measures to prevent risky behaviour among these groups, including awareness building, condom promotion, creation of an enabling environment and reinforcing traditional Indian moral values. The Policy advocates the provision of HIV/AIDS education in schools and colleges through curricular and extra-curricular activities, as well as through youth organisations for those outside of educational institutions (NACO, 2002).

The National Youth Policy 2003

The National Youth Policy 2003 addresses the needs of those aged between13–35. It especially recognizes adolescents (aged 13–19) as a special group requiring different strategies from those appropriate for young adults (aged 20–35). With regard to health issues, the Youth Policy outlines a number of the recommendations articulated in the National Population Policy and the National AIDS Prevention and Control Policy, and highlights several new strategies as well. The National Population Policy recognizes the vulnerability of youth in the sexual and reproductive health arena, and recommends the provision of counselling, services and information to enhance safe behaviours and to raise age at marriage. It also advocates the provision of free state-sponsored counselling services for youth, the establishment of "adolescent clinics" to provide appropriate counselling and treatment, and the establishment of Youth Health Associations at the grassroots level to provide family welfare and counselling services. As with the National Population Policy, the Youth Policy also reiterates the commitment to redress gender imbalances among young people in terms of age at marriage, nutritional status and life skills building. It also recognizes the need for a multi-sectoral focus on youth empowerment and gender justice. The policy placed adolescent health as a subsection under the health sector. Youth empowerment and gender justice were recognized as the major thrust areas of the policy (Government of India, 2003).

The National Policy on Education

The National Policy on Education emphasizes that educational programmes should actively motivate and inform adolescents about family planning and responsible parenthood. It also stresses the need to reduce gender imbalances in school attendance and completion (GOI, 1998).

The National Policy for the Empowerment of Women

The National Policy for the Empowerment of Women identifies adolescent girls as a vulnerable group and highlights the need to address their education and nutrition needs; at the same time it recognizes the need to raise age at marriage and address gender-based violence (GOI, 2001).

The National Health Policy 2002

The National Health Policy 2002 recognizes the need to address nutritional deficiencies in women and girls, and to raise awareness among school and college students about health promoting behaviour (GOI, 2002).

Tenth and Eleventh Plans

Tenth and Eleventh Plans the Five-Year Plans articulate the commitment to address the needs of adolescents and young people, particularly the tenth and eleventh Plans, and the National Adolescent Reproductive and Sexual Health Strategy provides the framework for the adolescent sexual and reproductive health services proposed in the RCH Programme II. The **Tenth Plan** document recognised adolescents as a group with special and distinct needs and underscored the importance of investing in adolescents. It proposed launching a new scheme aimed at sensitising adolescents about an array of issues including safe motherhood, reproductive health rights, sexuality and sexual responsibility, age at marriage and first pregnancy, hygiene, immunization, HIV/AIDS prevention and the importance of education, particularly of girls, as well as providing some legal literacy and information about vocational opportunities and career planning. It also proposed to implement nutrition and health interventions for adolescent girls (Planning Commission, 2002).

Eleventh Five Year Plan

Eleventh Plan approach paper recognised that adolescent girls remain marginalised, and seeks to focus on reducing the incidence of anemia and malnutrition among adolescent girls to break the cycle of ill-health and maternal and infant mortality. The approach paper also promoted awareness about gender issues among youth using the Panchayat Yuva Shakthi Abhiyan (Planning Commission, 2006).

National Adolescent Reproductive and Sexual Health Strategy (ARSH) under RCH-II

National Adolescent Reproductive and Sexual Health Strategy (ARSH) under RCH-II is the most comprehensive in terms of addressing adolescent's sexual and reproductive health needs. This strategy has recognized, the heterogeneity of adolescents, including married and unmarried. It calls on the health sector to provide friendly, confidential and non-judgemental services for adolescents, proposes detailed training of various providers to enhance their ability to serve adolescent's needs, and advocates a wider range of services for adolescents (GOI, 2006).

Several policies formulated at the national level articulate a commitment to meet the sexual and reproductive health needs of adolescents. Except the recent National Adolescent Reproductive and Sexual Health Strategy, most policies have overlooked the fact that adolescents are not a homogenous group.

The National Population Policy has neglected to discuss whether it is advocating services for all adolescents or exclusively for married adolescents. While it does not specifically indicate that unmarried adolescents are ineligible to access services, such statements as "reproductive health services for adolescent girls and boys are especially significant in rural India, where adolescent marriage and pregnancy are widely prevalent" suggest a certain ambivalence with regard to the extent to which services will be made available to meet the sexual and reproductive health needs of the unmarried.

The National Youth Policy remains ambiguous about the extent to which services will be made available to the unmarried girls.

The focus of the National AIDS Prevention and Control Policy 2002 is largely on unmarried young people (students in school and college) and to a certain extent, married young men. Even though the Policy advocates reaching out-of-school youth, who obviously include both the unmarried and married, through networks of youth organisations, sports clubs, the National Service

Scheme and Nehru Yuvak Kendras, the fact that most of these networks largely cater to young males suggests that unmarried out-of-school and married adolescent girls and young women are unlikely to be able to make use of the proposed programmes.

While almost all policies underscore the need to raise awareness about sexual and reproductive health issues among adolescents, many do not recognise adolescents' need for sexual and reproductive health services. The National AIDS Prevention and Control Policy is notably silent about the delivery of any specially packaged services for adolescents. The National Health Policy does not contain any reference to adolescents' need for sexual and reproductive health services or counselling. Further, policies that have recognised such needs are somewhat ambiguous about the nature of services to be made available to adolescents.

The focus of the National Population Policy is clearly on the less controversial aspects of sexual and reproductive health, counselling and dissemination of information—but not quite as clearly on the provision of services to unmarried adolescents. In this Policy, adolescents are included as a target audience for community-level education campaigns about the availability of safe abortion services and the dangers of unsafe abortion, but they are not included as a target group for safe and legal abortion services.

The National Youth Policy remains silent about the kinds of services that the recommended adolescent clinics and programmes will provide and the extent to which services will be available to the unmarried girls.

The National Population Policy and the National Youth Policy do not adequately recognize the barriers that adolescents face in accessing sexual and reproductive health services. For example, affordability and accessibility are issues that are merely cited but not discussed in the National Population Policy, and issues of confidentiality are also neither mentioned nor discussed. While, the National Youth Policy mentions these issues, it does not discuss how confidentiality or quality of care will be addressed. This gap has however been recognized, and the National Adolescent Reproductive and Sexual Health Strategy clearly notes both the need for confidentiality and youth-friendly care (GOI, 2006).

Given the lack of recognition at policy level of adolescents' need for sexual and reproductive health services, it is not surprising that the need for orienting health care providers about adolescents' service needs have not been discussed in most policies, including the National Population Policy, the National Youth Policy and the National AIDS Prevention and Control Policy. The National Adolescent Reproductive and Sexual Health Strategy is an exception, emphasising the need for provider orientation and training and even training guides for different levels of the health care system (GOI, 2006).

Most of the policies for the adolescents are dedicated to address the gender disparities underlying the poor sexual and reproductive health situation of adolescents. However, the policy documents are not clear about how these commitments are to be operationalised. Further, while reference is made to the need to create a safe environment to address adolescents' needs, the measures to be taken to do so are rarely described in policy documents.

National Programmes related to Reproductive Health of the Adolescents

Government and nongovernment organizations (NGOs) have initiated various programmes as a part of the strategy to implement policies. These programmes to translate policies for adolescents into reality were mainly initiated in the 1980s. Since the 1990s programmatic efforts in the area of sexual and reproductive health have been considerably enhanced. These programme initiatives have also received support from regional and international organizations and agencies. Most of the NGO programmes are supported by funding as well as by technical assistance. These support organizations include governments, NGOs, and international organizations in addition to government ministries and departments. Among the major international and bilateral organizations are: UNFPA, UNICEF, UNESCO, WHO, World Bank, and DANIDA. The range of programmes varies because of organizations' varying experiences and capacities to undertake adolescent related issues.

National Population Education Programme (NPEP)

The earliest and most well known programme to be initiated in the country was the National Population Education Programme, currently known as the Population and Development Education Programme. Launched in the early 1980s and implemented through schools, colleges and non-formal adult education centres, the National Population Education Programme originally aimed to sensitise young people with regard to population and development issues. With the paradigm shift in the 1990s, the National Population Education Programme shifted its focus from demographic issues to reproductive and sexual health and gender issues (Chakrabarti 2003). To further national efforts to promote family life and population education among adolescents, the National Centre for Educational Research and Training (NCERT), which is responsible for developing national curriculum standards, has incorporated sex education with information on the growth and development of adolescents, life skills and HIV/AIDS into the national curriculum since the mid-1990s. The NPEP has been institutionalized as part of the Government of India's Tenth Five Year Plan.

School AIDS Education Programme

With the emergence of the HIV epidemic, the Ministry of Human Resource

Development, Department of Education and the National AIDS Control Organisation have launched a number of HIV/AIDS education programmes in schools. The School AIDS Education Programme for example has been established for students of Classes IX–XII. As part of the programme, a generic toolkit has been prepared for implementation at the state level, which includes a Learning for Life module as well as training and advocacy materials, teachers' workbooks and flip charts, reference books, booklets on Frequently Asked Questions for students and a 40-hour life skills programme. Sessions are generally conducted in the biology or science class, and include such topics as human anatomy and modes of HIV transmission, prevention and testing. The "Youth Unite for Victory on AIDS" campaign, launched in June 2006 by the Ministry of Youth Affairs and Sports and NACO in collaboration with seven National Youth Organisations, also intends to strengthen ongoing efforts to raise sexual and reproductive health awareness among school-going students.

Reproductive and Child Health (RCH) Services Programme

The RCH Programme was launched nationwide in 1996 to provide holistic reproductive and child health care through the existing, vast network of the primary health care system. The RCH Programme encompasses provisions for all aspects of safe motherhood and child survival interventions, including a focus on increased access to contraceptives, safe management of unwanted pregnancies, enhanced nutrition, prevention and management of Reproductive Tract Infections (RTIs) and Sexually Transmitted Infections (STIs), availability of reproductive health services to adolescents, and educational outreach. The RCH Programme also focuses on providing services for gynecological problem management and cancer screening for women. The programme has been in operation since 1996 and is being monitored through periodic nationwide, district based Rapid Household Surveys.

RCH Programe II (2005)

The RCH Implementation Guide for State and District Programme Managers prepared by the Ministry of Health and Family Welfare also proposes to strengthen health education activities in schools for adolescents as part of the RCH Programme II. Auxiliary nurse midwives (ANMs) and male health workers are expected to conduct monthly group communication activities in schools, and occasionally attend health education sessions in schools and provide appropriate inputs. Medical officers from primary health centres are expected to conduct health check-ups once in six months in schools and inform adolescents about the availability of services (GOI, 2006).

National AIDS Control Programme (NACP-III-2005),

National AIDS Control Programme (NACP-III-2005), calls for a comprehensive approach to reach young people especially highly vulnerable groups. The overall focus of this five- year plan is on AIDS education, condom promotion, and the establishment of an improved blood tansfusion system, among other areas. The adolescent Education Programme, University talks AIDS, Villages Talks AIDS, Red Ribbon Clubs and Link workers scheme are a few initiatives that have been specifically designed for adolescents, young people and women who otherwise are often missed out in the HIV education drive.

National Adolescence Education Programme

National Adolescence Education Programme, a collaborative effort by MHRD and NACO is aimed at providing adolescents authentic knowledge about process of growing up during adolescence, HIV/AIDS and substance abuse, helping them inculcate positive attitude towards these issues and developing in them life skills, so that they are capable to manage risky situations and challenges of life.

YUVA School Adolescence Education Programme (SAEP)

Directorate of Education in collaboration with Delhi State AIDS Control Society (DSACS) has initiated School Adolescence Education Programme (SAEP) titled "YUVA". It seeks to sensitize adolescents about a range of issues confronting them at different stages of their growing up. It includes scholastic and career plan, generic life skills, growing up and health and hygiene, body image and nutrition, interpersonal relationship and effective communication, mental health and substance abuse, adolescents' sexual and reproductive health. It can be noticed that sexual and reproductive health is one of the area along with other components. In the first phase they have targeted only governments schools in Delhi and later on it will reach out unaided and aided private schools and out of school students (Directorate of Education, 2009 a).

YUVA Phone Line

YUVA phone line 1800116888 a project of Department of Education and Delhi State AIDS Control Society lines open from 11am to 5 pm. Counselors are available there on all working days to talk to adolescents to offer guidance and support. Parents too can ring up and seek advice (Directorate of Education, 2009 b).

Baika Samriddhi Yojana, 1997

This scheme works to raise the status of girl children born in families below the poverty line by providing financial help to these families. Some specific criteria have been laid down to provide financial assistance to the mother of a newborn girl child in the form of grants and investments through a postal financial instrument to be applied toward the education and economic independence of that child. The scheme also provides a scholarship provision for the girl's school education. The deposit will mature and be paid to the girl if she remains unmarried until she reaches 18 years of age. More than two million girls have benefited from the scheme so far.

Several other initiatives that have been taken to promote the development of adolescents include the following:

- The National Service Scheme (NSS) was launched in 1969 with a primary focus on students' personality development and community service. NSS involved more than 1.6 million student volunteers from more than 175 universities and 22 senior secondary councils. The scheme's programmes include "regular activities" and "special campaign programmes."
- *Bharat* Scouts and Guides, the third largest youth organization in the world, has enrolled 2.3 million guides and scouts. Scouting and guiding movements aim to develop boys' and girls' characters with the goal of making them good citizens of India. It inculcates in them a spirit of patriotism and promotes balanced physical and mental development.

Population Council

The Population Council has supported initiatives on adolescent transition in different states in collaboration with several NGOs, namely RUWSEC in Tamil Nadu, SUTRA in Himachal Pradesh, ADITHI in Bihar, CINI in West Bengal, and CHETNA in Gujarat and Rajasthan (Population Council, 1999). The Population Council supported programmes on adolescence run by Mahila Samakhya in Karnataka and Andhra Pradesh and in the state of Haryana, *Apni Beti Aapna Dhan*.

Prerana

Prerana initiated adolescent programmes in 1987 and in 1990, Prerana further enhanced its initiatives by launching the Better Life Demonstration Project for Girls and Young Women and a parallel programme of Better Life Development Programme for Boys and Young Men. The objective of each programme is to create an environment of dignity and opportunity for adolescents, enabling them to achieve their full potential in terms of personal growth and ability to contribute to family, community, and societal development. The programmes were implemented as a development project in six villages along the periphery of Delhi. The programme targeted individuals and their peer groups, families, and communities. Learning modules included information, education, and services in the areas of personality development, education, health, reproductive health, economic participation, and life skills training. Over 5,000 adolescent girls and 1,800 adolescent boys have been reached through direct field programmes (Population Council, 1999).

Pathfinder/India

Pathfinder's adolescent health programme work in partnership with Indian NGOs, initially focusing on the provision of reproductive health information, education, counseling, and services for adolescents.

Centre for Development and Population Activities (CEDPA)

CEDPA, an international NGO with operations in Delhi, in collaboration with local NGOs, UNFPA, UNESCO and USAID, has adopted "Choose a Future: Issues and Options for Adolescent Boys" and "Choose a Future: Issues and Options for Adolescent Girls" to the Indian cultural context and is currently implementing programmes in 11 states. The package has been designed to effectively challenge gender inequalities and address male involvement. It helps to foster true partnerships in relationships, responsible fatherhood, and alternatives to violence.

Planned Parenthood Federation

Planned Parenthood has promoted four major projects with the help of local NGOs:

- *Improving the Reproductive Health of Young Women and Men*: The goal of the project is to improve the lives of adolescents and youth by providing contraceptive services and sexuality education in 20 rural villages in a district in West Bengal with a local NGO.
- *Couple to Couple: Improving the Reproductive Health of Young Couples in Rural India:* The project employs peer couples to work with groups of newlyweds and other young couples to motivate them to increase gender awareness, encourage supportive relationships, and plan for their new families together. The aim of this project is to create an enabling environment for young couples to overcome social, cultural, and gender barriers to plan and space their children's births and achieve positive reproductive and child health.
- *Improving the Reproductive Health of Adolescents and Youth*: Located in Jharkhand state, the project aims to increase young people's knowledge and understanding about sexuality and reproductive health and help them develop communication and decision-making skills so that they may lead healthy reproductive lives.
- *Reproductive Health through Advocacy and Services*: The project is

a part of a larger programme to improve the reproductive health and rights of adolescents and youth in the Indian states of Bihar and West Bengal. The programme aims to improve the general reproductive health of adolescents and young people and develop the capacity of NGOs, private providers, and government facilities to plan, sustain, and advocate for adolescent and youth reproductive health programmes.

From above it is evident that various approaches have been adopted to raise awareness about sexual and reproductive health among adolescents, and that programmes have been implemented for the adolescents. While these programmatic initiatives are commendable, many are poorly implemented; moreover, their impact has not been properly evaluated and assessments of coverage and quality or effectiveness differ. As of 2005, the Adolescent Education Programme has been implemented in only slightly more than two-fifths of secondary schools nationally (NACO, MOHFW, and GOI, 2005). It has been reported that feedback from students who attended the programme was generally positive and the opportunity to explore sexual matters in a safe space appreciated by both girls and boys, it is evident that adolescents are interested in receiving more explicit information, for example, how to use a condom (NACO, MOHFW, and GOI, 2005).

Access to information through television programmes, telephone helplines and to a lesser extent radio programmes is likely to be limited among young women, particularly the married, who typically have restricted freedom of movement or decision-making authority within the home. Finally, the recently initiated information provision activities to be conducted under the RCH Programme II by ANMs and male workers are expected to be held on a monthly basis in schools, among adolescent's groups, in villages and urban areas, and among recently-married couples, but again, it is unlikely that recently-married women will have the mobility or decision-making authority to attend group meetings in most settings.

With regard to the content of programmes, the themes addressed are generic and rarely modified to suit the unique needs of different groups of adolescents. The various programmes relating to HIV/AIDS tend to focus on the nature of the disease, and the modes of transmission and prevention, including the role of condoms. Those relating to reproductive health address more generally contraception and pregnancy-related care. The topics that are particularly suitable to the young such as opposite or same-sex relationships and sex, how condoms are to be used and appropriate contraceptive methods for young people (for example, emergency contraception and condoms) are not covered. While HIV and condom use are stressed, programmes make little effort to raise awareness of other sexually transmitted infections (STIs). Reproductive health education conducted, at the school level, also tends to be technical (for example, human anatomy or modes of HIV transmission) and such key issues as sexuality, sexual behaviour and gender relations are not explicitly covered.

Although policies and programmes in India have underscored the rights of adolescents to sexual and reproductive health counselling and services, service delivery has not been adolescents-friendly or responsive to their unique needs. Compared to awareness raising programmes, sexual and reproductive health counselling and services are provided overwhelmingly through the RCH Programme; AIDS control programmes play a smaller role in providing services to young people (Manju, 2006).

The RCH Programme II represents a major shift from earlier programmes in that it is more inclusive, addressing the needs of different groups of young people. The National Programme Implementation Plans (PIP) have outlined a two-pronged strategy by which to meet adolescent needs: first, incorporating specific activities to reach adolescents within sexual and reproductive health services intended for adults more generally; and second, providing services specifically intended for adolescents at the primary health centre level on dedicated days and at dedicated times. These special services are to be initiated in certain districts, to be selected on the basis of such indicators as low age at marriage and high prevalence of adolescent pregnancy (GOI, 2006).

Conclusion

This Chapter has explored the major policies and programmes related to the sexual and reproductive health of adolescents in India, and assessed the extent to which these efforts have responded to adolescents' needs. Above discussion reflects that several programmes have been undertaken that attempt to reach to the adolescents both through the RCH Programme II and through HIV awareness building activities. While these programmatic initiatives are commendable, the study suggests that many remain poorly implemented, may not reach all groups of adolescents, and little is known about their impact or quality. Of particular concern is the finding that out-of-school and married females may not be reached as they are unlikely to be members of clubs or *mandals*, or to have access to television programmes or telephone hotlines, and may not have the mobility or decision-making authority to attend group meetings in most settings.

There is a need to put efforts to integrate adolescents' diverse concerns more directly into programmes. While the expansion of the scope of the RCH Programme II and the responsibilities of health workers to include provision of sexual and reproductive health services, including contraceptives, to the unmarried is a significant step forward, the extent to which services have been expanded in reality is not yet clear. Efforts must be made to ensure that providers at health and voluntary counselling and testing facilities deliver sensitive, non-judgmental, private and confidential services to adolescents. The roles and responsibilities of male health workers must be redefined to include sexual and reproductive health counselling and the provision of services to adolescents. The establishment of regular adolescent health clinics at the primary health centre and community health centre level, highlighted in the RCH Programme II, is a positive move but needs to be urgently implemented and its ability to attract adolescents carefully monitored.

Despite the fact that reproductive health programmes related to adolescents have noted the importance of sensitising gatekeepers (parents and teachers), efforts have been limited in terms of the number of activities undertaken, the kinds of gatekeepers addressed and the extent to which programme content is intended to orient gatekeepers to adolescents' needs or to enable gatekeepers to overcome their own discomfort and misconceptions about addressing sexual and reproductive matters among adolescents. Parents are rarely included in gatekeeper programmes, although the importance of parent-child communication has been frequently stressed. Teacher training has not succeeded in enabling teachers to overcome their own embarrassment in dealing with these issues.

In a nutshell, the policies and programmes, be they related to women and child development, youth, health and family welfare or HIV/AIDS, have all recognized the importance of improving sexual and reproductive health of the adolescents. Efforts have been initiated for the same, as evident from recently introduced strategies to enhance the sexual and reproductive health of adolescents; what is needed is a similar level of commitment to ensure that programmes do reach to adolescents, that it should be implemented properly in an effective way.

4

Adolescents, Parents, and Teachers—Profiles

In order to understand the overall situation or context of a particular group of people in a particular setting, it is very important to understand their demographic characteristics. This chapter presents the profile of the adolescents, parents and teachers.

Demographic Characteristics of Adolescents in India

Demography is a scientific, statistical study of the human population. "Demas" means "the people", "Grapho" means, "to draw or write". This means demography is all about drawing or writing about people. According to Webster's Dictionary, Demography is the statistical study of human populations, a specially their size and distribution the number of births and deaths. According to Oxford's Dictionary, Demography is the study of statistics of births, deaths, disease, etc., as illustrating conditions of life in communities.

***Adolescent Population*:** As on March 2001, adolescents accounted for 22.8 per cent of the population of India (Figure 4.1).

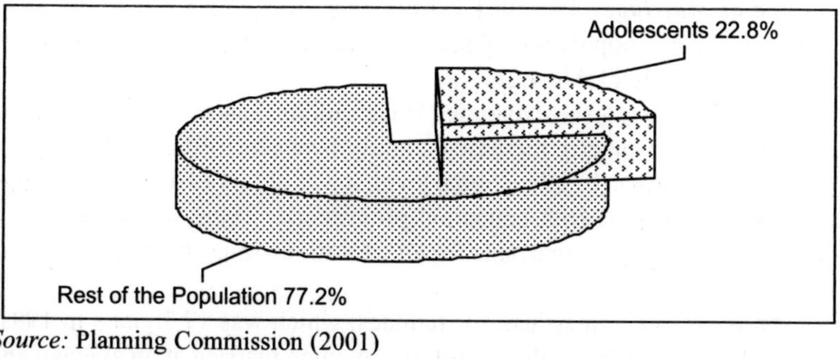

Source: Planning Commission (2001)

Figure 4.1: Proportion of Adolescents in Total Population of India

There are around 239 million adolescents in India in the age group of 10-19 years presently. Over the next two decades the number of adolescents is likely to increase further but their share to population will decrease marginally as per the projections (Planning Commission 2001).

Sex Ratio: According to the 2001 Census, the sex ratio is 933 females per 1000 males a disturbing indicator of gender discrimination. The strong preference for a male child, which manifests itself in the form of sex selective abortions, infanticide, malnutrition, neglect and exploitation of girls and women, is a major cause behind the adverse sex ratio.

Table 4.1 Sex Ratio by Age Group 1981–2001

Age-group	*Sex Ratio (Females per 1000 males)*		
	1981	*1991*	*2001*
All ages	934	927	933
10-14	898	900	902
15-19	885	871	858

Source: Rajiv Gandhi National Institute for Youth Development (2007 a)

The sex ratio for adolescents in the 15-19 years age group declined from around 885 girls per 1000 boys in 1981 to 871 girls in 1991, and 858 girls in 2001. The predominance of males is notable among adolescents. The patriarchal structure with preference for male children affects intra familial food distribution and selective health consultation for male children which may result in higher childhood and adolescent mortality in children.

***Marriage/Nuptial Patterns*:** According to the 1929 Child Marriage Act, the legal minimum age for marriage is 21 years for men and 18 years for women. While the Act imposes penalties for any violation of its provisions, it has not affected the practice of early marriage. Marriages below the legal age remain prevalent in the country.

***Age at Marriage*:** The 2001 census data are compared with the 1991 census on married population by sex and mean age at marriage for different levels of education. (Table 4.2)

Data on age at marriage recorded in Census 2001 show that the mean age at marriage in the country increased slightly between 1991 and 2001 by 0.6 years. On comparison by educational level, it was observed that the mean age at marriage increased with education progression. There was also a trend toward increasing age at marriage for all education groups between 1991 and 2001.

The mean age at marriage for females, which was 17.7 years in 1991, increased to 18.3 in 2001. While illiterate women married at an average age of 17.6 years, the mean age was 22.6 years for those who were graduates and

Table 4.2: Mean Age at Marriage (Years) for Currently Married Population by Sex and Educational Level, 1991 and 2001

Educational Level	*1991*		*2001*		*Increase in Mean Age at Marriage (MAM) (years) 1991-2001 for Females*
	Male	*Female*	*Male*	*Female*	
Total	NA	17.7	22.6	18.3	0.6
Illiterate	NA	17.2	21.6	17.6	0.4
Literate	NA	18.6	23.0	19.2	0.6
Literate but below primary	NA	–	22.4	18.1	–
Primary but below middle	NA	17.9	22.3	18.4	0.5
Middle but below matric or secondary	NA	18.5	22.4	19.1	0.5
Matric or secondary but below graduate	NA	19.7	23.4	20.2	0.5
Graduate and above	NA	21.5	25.3	22.6	1.1

Note: (1) For 1991, Mean age at marriage is not calculated for males, as tabulation of data by age and marriage for males was not done during Census 1991.
(2) Figures for 1991 exclude Jammu and Kashmir since census was not conducted there due to disturbed conditions.

Source: Census (2001), United Nations Population Fund (2005)

above—a difference of more than four years. In the case of males, the mean age at marriage was 22.6 years and the difference by education was similar to that of women. Substantial increases in mean age of marriage occurred after they attained matric or secondary level of education

***Marital Status*:** Table 4.3 presents the per cent distribution of marital status of adolescents (10-19 years) in 2001. Based on the tables, the proportion of those who were married among the adolescents (ages 10-19) for males and females were 6.1 per cent and 26.8 per cent, respectively. Females tended to marry earlier.

Table 4.3: Marital Status of Adolescents (10–19 years), 2001

Age-group	*Males*				*Females*			
	NM	*M*	*W*	*D/S*	*NM*	*M*	*W*	*D/S*
10-14	99.00	0.91	0.04	0.07	97.44	2.38	0.13	0.04
15-19	94.68	5.20	0.06	0.05	75.14	24.45	0.20	0.20

Note: NM = Never married, M = Married, W = Widowed, D/S = Divorced/Separated

Source: Census (2001), Rajiv Gandhi National Institute for Youth Development (2007 b)

By far, there were more married females 10-19 than males (a gap of 20.7%). It emphasized that early marriage violates a number of rights (please refer Figure 4.2) of the girl and inhibits her holistic development.

Early marriage of girls undermines a number of rights guaranteed by the *Convention on the Fights of the Child.*

- The right to education (Article 28)
- The right to be protected from all forms of physical or mental violence, injury or abuse, including sexual abuse (Article 19) and from all forms of sexual exploitation (Article 34).
- The right to the enjoyment of the highest attainable standard of health (Article 24)
- The right to educational and vocational information and guidance (Article 28).
- The right to seek, receive and impart information and ideas (Article 13)
- The right to rest and leisure, and to participate freely in cultural life (Article 31)
- The right to not be separated from their parents against their will (Article 9)
- The right to protection against all forms of exploitation affecting any aspect of the child's welfare (Article 36)

Source: United Nations Population Fund (2003).

Figure 4.2: Rights Denied by Child Marriage or Early Marriage

Early marriage has far reaching consequences in terms of the development of adolescent boys and girls, their fertility rate and reproductive health. Marriage curtails education and alters their choice of careers. Teenage pregnancy poses risk to both infants and mother. If girls who are not fully developed become pregnant, they can experience damage to their reproductive tracts, delayed or obstructed labour, rupture in the birth canal and increased risks of maternal mortality. Also teenage parents lack experience, skills and resources needed to raise their children.

Adolescent Students

This section deals with the profile of the adolescent students studying between classes IX-XII in a co-educational government or private school in the National Capital Territory of Delhi. The information on background of the adolescents is based on the interviews conducted with 320 students, care has been taken to give equal representation to the adolescents according to their class, gender, and type of school.

***Age*:** In Delhi, students are admitted to schools at lower kindergarten class at the age of minimum three plus years or in the first standard at a minimum age of five plus years. So by the time the student finishes schooling 10+2, the student completes a minimum of 17 years in school. In the present study the overall age of the respondents varied between 12-20 years. For the purpose of generating more specific data on the age of the respondents, the age of the respondents was grouped into two categories viz., age between

12-16 years and 16-20 years. The findings reflect that the adolescents in the age group of 12-16 years were 60 per cent while in the age group of 16- 20 years were 40 per cent. The average age of the respondents in both types of schools was found to be approximately 16 years.

Class, Type of School, and Gender: According to Central Board of Secondary Examination (2009), 2,31,651 students had registered for the Secondary School Examination (X class) in Delhi. At the Senior School Certificate Examination (Class XII), 1,81,393 students had registered for the examination. In the present study the adolescent students were drawn from the senior classes of the school. The sample size consisted 320 students i.e., 160 students (80 girls and 80 boys) from each stratum (government and private schools). The table 4.4 shows the equal representation of the adolescent students according to their class, type of school and gender.

Table 4.4: Class wise Distribution of adolescent students (Type of School and Gender)

Class	*School Type*					
	Government			*Private*		
	Gender		*Total*	*Gender*		*Total*
	Female	*Male*		*Female*	*Male*	
IX-X	40	40	80 (50.00%)	40	40	80 (50.00%)
XI–XII	40	40	80 (50.00%)	40	40	80 (50.00%)
Total	80 (50.00%)	80 (50.00%)	160 (100.00%)	80 (50.00%)	80 (50.00%)	160 (100.00%)

Religion: The data on religion of the adolescent students was collected on the basis of four major religious communities existing in India viz., Hindu, Muslim, Sikh, and Christian community. None of the respondent belonged to Christian community. The religion wise distribution of data reflects that a large majority (94.38%) of the adolescent students were Hindus. The other religions adolescent students belonged to were Islam and Sikhism.

Family Details: To understand students, it is important to understand the families they come from. Family is the basic unit of the society. The key function of family is to raise its young persons in as healthy a manner as possible. Children are said to be the products of their parent's socialization methods. Socialization between parent and children for many years was viewed as a one-way process. But today parent-child interaction is viewed as reciprocal. Reciprocal socialization is a socialization process that is bi-directional; children socialize parents just as parents socialize children (Grouter and Booth, 2003; Patterson and Fisher, 2002).

Type of Family: The type of family can be classified into three category viz., nuclear, joint and single parent. The nuclear family for the purpose of the study has been considered constituting father, mother, and the children. The joint family comprised more than one nuclear family residing together in the same household i.e., grandparents, parents, children, uncle-aunt and their children. The single parent family considered to be a family with the presence of one of the parent either mother or father. Data showed that nearly equal number of adolescent students from government and private schools belonged to nuclear, joint and single parent family. In entirety half of the adolescent students were from nuclear family, 46 per cent from joint and 4 per cent lived in single parent families.

Size of the Family: In this study the adolescent students' family size varied from three members to nine members, therefore the average number of members of household (mean) can not be calculated. It was observed that less than 1.9 per cent adolescent students were two siblings in a single parent family. The respondents were regrouped to divide the families into two groups. It was found that 18.1 per cent students came from small families with four or less than four members. Majority (81.9%) of the students came from large families with five or more than five members.

Number of Siblings: Siblings are more accessible to each other and can play an important role in shaping and influencing each others' life. Sibling relationship includes helping, sharing, role modeling, fighting and playing. Siblings are close to each others' age and can understand each other's problems and communicate more effectively than parents can, in different situations like dealing with peers, coping with difficult situations, discussing taboo subjects as sex. In brief siblings seem to be more influential than parents in the socialization process. The number of siblings in a family throws some light to the family environment of the students. Is the respondent the only child? Or is a member in a large family? These cause differences in the environment of the students.

The distribution of respondents by the number of their siblings and type of school shows that the siblings of the respondents of both government and private schools were virtually equal in numbers. The findings reflect that 28.8 per cent of the respondents were having one or no siblings. The category with the highest respondents (66.3%) was students with 2-3 siblings. While another group of (5%) respondents had 4-5 siblings. The average no. of siblings in both types of schools was found to be 2 siblings.

Socioeconomic Status: Socioeconomic status (SES) refers to the grouping of people with similar occupational, educational and economic characteristics. The inequalities in the socioeconomic status produce unequal opportunities for students (Santrock, 2004). The families, schools and neighborhood of students have socioeconomic characteristics. The samples in this research were taken from all types of schools; different socio-economic status groups are represented. It includes parents of respondents from the illiterate or lower educational class to highly qualified professionals.

Educational Qualifications of the Parents of the Adolescent Students

The level of education of the parents of adolescents may affect adolescents' health in general and reproductive health in particular. The educational status of the parents of the adolescent students was assessed on the basis of their academic qualification which was classified into five categories viz., illiterate, upto 12th, graduation, post-graduation, and N.A. (Not Applicable).

Like fathers, the mothers of the adolescent students too had diverse educational backgrounds. Some mothers had not gone to school at all, while some were postgraduates. Overall analysis of the findings show that 9 of the parents (both mother and father) were illiterate, 86 studied upto 12th, 89 graduates, and 7 post-graduates.

Occupational Status of the Parents of the Adolescent Students: The occupational structure of the respondents is an important indicator of the socio-economic situation. Occupation of the parents of the adolescent students was listed to understand the nature of work the earners of the family were engaged in.

Data Reflects that fathers of the adolescent students were involved in different occupations. A small number of fathers (5%) were daily wage earners. In this group of daily wagers, nearly 95 per cent of their wards mainly went to government schools. 18.8 per cent of the fathers were in government service while one fourth (25.3%) of the fathers were in private service. A small percentage of the fathers were self- employed professionals. The respondents' fathers were daily wagers, pulling rickshaw or doing unskilled work, others were into business, service sector or self- employed professionals.

The largest numbers of adolescent students' mothers (83.4%) were housewives. Among the adolescent students' mothers who were employed, a small group (1.3%) constituted daily wage earners. 3.8 per cent of the mothers were into government services while 9.4 per cent were into private services. Another group (1.3%) of mothers was engaged in business and only one of the adolescent student's mother was self employed professional.

Monthly Income of the Family: Family income has an impact on the health and nutrition status of the households, especially on adolescents. Family income is also an important variable that reflects SES (Socioeconomic Status) of the respondents. The adolescent students in the study came from different income groups. The monthly family income ranged from ₹ 5000 and below to maximum family income in the group of ₹ 25000 and above.

Data depicts that a low per cent 6.56 per cent of the respondents' had a monthly family income of below ₹ 5000. A small group (1.8%) of these respondents mentioned that many a times their fathers would not get work as they were rickshaw pullers and they would have no money at home. There were 3 (0.46%) respondents who specifically mentioned their monthly family income was above rupees one lakh, therefore average income of the family (mean) per month was not calculated.

Parents

Parents strongly influence their wards. Parents play a crucial role in the growth and development of their wards. Students need the security that only their own parents can give them. They need the feeling of confidence that comes from parental faith. They also need supervision, direction and firm setting of limits. As adolescents move toward independence, they experience resistance. Parents need to understand the adolescents' needs and problems and in helping the next generation to emerge confident.

This section deals with the profile of the parents of the adolescents. Only those parents formed a part of this study whose children studying between class IX-XII in a co-educational government or private schools. In the National Capital Territory of Delhi and were willing to participate in the research. Total 40 parents were interviewed, 10 from each school selected for the study. It is to be noted that Parents were also asked separately on educational qualification, occupation and monthly family income.

Age: It is to be noted that the respondents (respondents in this section mean the parents of the adolescents) interviewed on the days they came for the PTM (Parent Teachers meeting) hence total nine fathers and 31 mothers were interviewed.

Average age of fathers and mothers calculated were 41 and 39 years respectively. Not much variation in the age of the parents seen in the findings on the basis of type of schools.

Educational Qualification: The data on educational qualification of the respondents (parents of the adolescent students) was collected on the basis of four categories viz., illiterate, upto 12th, graduation, and post- graduation. It can be noted from the data that only 2 mothers were illiterate while in case of fathers among 9, one is illiterate. Rest of the parents was studied upto 12th, graduation or post-graduation.

Occupation: Occupation of the respondents was listed to understand the nature of work the parents of the adolescents was engaged in. Data on distribution of parents according to their occupation reflected that 7.5 per cent of the respondents engaged in government service. 15 per cent of the respondents engaged in the private service. 10 per cent of the respondents engaged in business while 7.5 per cent were daily wage earners. Data reflects that maximum mothers were housewives.

Monthly Family Income: Monthly family income is an important indicator to assess the family's economic state. Monthly family income was assessed categorizing into four categories viz., ₹ 5000 and below, 5001-10000, 10001-15000, 15001-20000, 20001-25000, and 25001 and above. Data depicts that 7.5 per cent of the respondents' had a monthly family income of below ₹5000, it is to be noted that they belonged to the daily wage earners category. Another 7.5 per cent of the respondents' family income was ₹5001 to 10000 and their wards attended government schools. The respondents' (35%) whose family income was 20001-25000 and as high as ₹25001 and above, most of them (32.50%) attended private schools. Average income of the family per month could not be calculated.

Teachers

This Section deals with the profile of the teachers of the adolescents. The teachers included in the study were teaching any of the classes between class IX-XII of a co-educational government or private schools in the National Capital Territory of Delhi and were willing to participate in the research. Total 40 teachers were interviewed, 10 from each (2 government and 2 private) school selected for the study.

Age: The Overall age of the respondents (respondents in this section mean the teachers of the government and private schools) varied between 22-62 years of age. The age of the respondents was grouped into four categories viz., 22-32 years, 32-42 years, 42-52 years, and 52-62 years. Data shows that 17.5 per cent of the respondents were from 22-32 years of the age group. 22.5 per cent respondents belonged to the age group of 32-42 years. 37.5 and 22.5 per cent of the respondents were from the age group of 42-52 and 52-62 years respectively. Overall analysis of the findings on age distribution of the teachers reflects that the average age of the teachers were 43.5 years. The average age of the private schools teachers was found to be little higher as compared to the teachers of government schools.

Educational Qualification: The educational background of the respondents was assessed on the basis of their academic qualification which was classified into three categories viz., B.A./B.Com/B.Sc-B.Ed., M.A./M.Com./M.Sc-B.Ed., and M.A.-M.Ed.

The distribution of the teachers according to their educational qualification revealed that all the teachers were having requisite qualification of the B.Ed. (Bachelors in Education)/M.Ed. (Masters in Education). The data also revealed that maximum (85%) teachers were Postgraduates and only 15 per cent were graduates.

Conclusion

This chapter elaborated on the background information of the adolescent students and their parents and teachers. An investigation was made into the profile of the adolescent students and their parents and teachers according to the type of the schools i.e., government and private schools, gender, class, age.

Profile of Adolescent Students: In the present study the adolescent students were drawn from the senior classes of the schools i.e. IX-X, and XI- XII class. The sample size consisted of 320 students. The equal representation has been given to the respondents according to their class, type of school and gender. The average age of the respondents was found to be 16 (15.6) years. A large majority (94.38%) of the respondents were Hindus. Nearly equal number of respondents from government and private schools belonged to nuclear, joint and single parent family. Respondents' family size varied from three members to nine members. Average number of siblings of the respondents was 2.025 (2 siblings). Both fathers the mothers of the respondents had diverse educational backgrounds. The data reflected that fathers of the respondents were involved in different occupations. Majority of the respondents' mothers (83.4%) were housewives. The family income ranges from below ₹5000 monthly to maximum family income in the group of ₹25000 and above.

Profile of the Parents: Average age of fathers and mothers calculated were 41 and 39 years respectively. It can be noted from the findings that only 2 mothers were illiterate while in case of fathers among 9, one is illiterate. Rest of the parents had studied upto 12th, Graduation or Post-Graduation. Data on distribution of parents according to their occupation reflected that maximum mothers were housewives.

Profile of the Teachers: The data on age distribution of the teachers reflected that the average age of the teachers were 43 years. The distribution of the teachers according to their educational qualification revealed that all the teachers were having requisite qualification of the B.Ed. (Bachelors in Education)/ M.Ed. (Masters in Education).

This chapter proved to be very beneficial to understand adolescent students', parents' and teachers' socio-economic and academic background. The students', parents' and teachers' views in detail on imparting reproductive health education will be studied in the further chapters.

5

Knowledge and Perception of Adolescents on Reproductive Health Issues

Knowledge means information and awareness gained through experience or education. Perception connotes a particular understanding of something or the process of perceiving. Perception is basic psychological process which serves as the means of acquiring experience or knowledge. It is the mental grasping of objects, events and persons through senses. Perception mainly includes learning and thinking. How the adolescent boys and girls perceive the world in their every day life experiences? The adolescent period is highly sensitive and critical one in which the adolescent boys and girls get easily frustrated, emotional and become maladjusted. False starts, mistakes, poor judgement, or impulsive action are part of growing up (Focus Adolescent Services, n.d.). The main task of adolescence requires them to learn, and this kind of learning is not just a matter of getting the right answer. Most important is to understand the meaning of right answer. And maybe "the right answer" is something that adolescents need to build up, responsibly, from lessons of experience. This is truly difficult and it absolutely requires education and support from parents and teachers. This chapter deals with the knowledge and perception of adolescent students on reproductive health issues.

Process of Growing Up

Adolescence is a time of rapid growth and development. During this period they attain reproductive and sexual maturity. Psychologically the adolescents are beset with various myths and misconceptions about physical changes. They are often confused and develop a sense of guilt about various body changes. When these changes are uneven, they are psychologically disturbed. Adolescents of the same age may have different stages of development. Different circumstances may make them face different problems and have different needs and beliefs (Dash, 2004).

As we know that the physiological changes are essential in the developmental process of human beings especially during adolescence. Some of these changes are common for boys and girls and some are gender specific, i.e. different for boys and girls therefore, this section is further divided in two sub-sections A and B namely: Process of growing up in Boys and, process of growing up in Girls.

Process of Growing up in Boys

Students' (boys') knowledge and perception were assessed on the process of growth and development during adolescence, such as physical growth and development including development of secondary sexual characteristics. Understanding the process of growing up is necessary as body image and rate of growth in relation to peers is a major concern of adolescents. Misconception about masturbation and nocturnal emission cause stress, social norms and inability to share their concerns with others make it even more stressful. It is very essential to make this transitory phase (adolescence) comfortable for the adolescent students so that they can cope with the pubertal changes in a healthy manner.

In this section 160 students (only boys) were interviewed, an equal number of students, i.e., 80 from each stratum (government and private schools) were interviewed.

Level of Awareness on Physiological Changes among Boys

Level of awareness of the adolescent boys was examined on physical changes they experienced. These included rapid gain in height and weight, growth of hairs in under arms, growth of hairs in pubic parts, appearance of hairs on the face, change in voice, nocturnal emission/ night fall. The above mentioned physical changes were assessed at three point scale, i.e., fully aware, partially aware, and not aware. Respondents' (boys) responses on level of awareness on physiological changes were cross tabulated with their class and type of school.

The analysis of the findings reflect that a significant number of students (boys) from both government and private schools were partially aware, i.e., 75 per cent and 77.5 per cent respectively. The partial awareness of the respondents implies that the knowledge and information they have on physiological changes was half – baked (which they may or may not know was accurate). The incorrect information can lead to misinterpretation and misuse. It was noteworthy to observe that 10 per cent students from each school government and private were not at all aware about the physiological changes hence they were more vulnerable. Overall analysis of data reveals that there is no significant difference in the level of awareness on the physiological changes among government and private school students.

Source of Information on Physiological Changes Experienced by Boys

The respondents (boys) were asked about the source of information they accessed to know about the physiological changes. Friends, siblings, mother, father, teacher, counselor, doctor, and do not discuss were considered as sources of information on physiological changes. For each source of information, data have been collected from the 160 respondents (80 boys each from government and private school). Each respondent could give more than one response as this was a multiple response question. Only the affirmative responses for each source of information on physiological changes were considered in the figure 5.1.

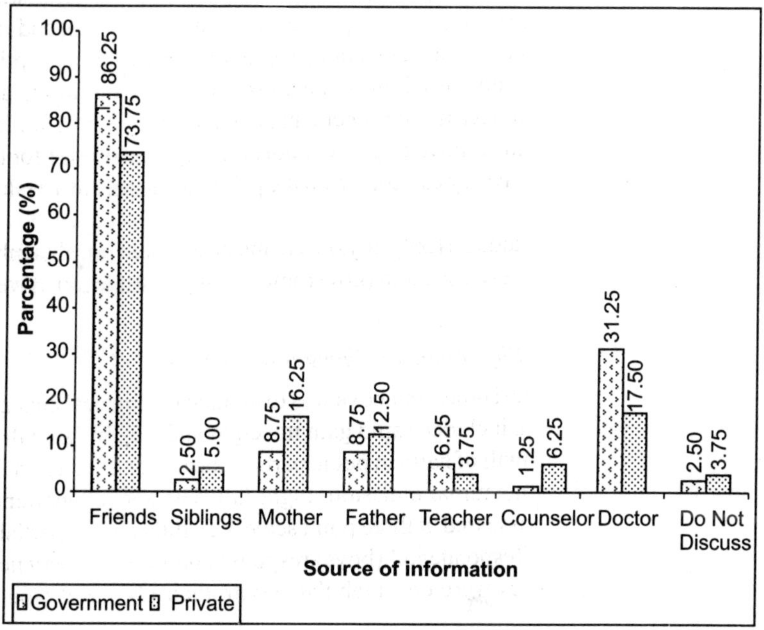

N = 80 (each type of school)

Figure 5.1: Source of Information Accessed by Boys on Physiological Changes

The findings illustrate that the friends (86.25% and 73.75% from government and private schools respectively) were considered more appropriate source in discussing on physiological changes as compared to the other sources. Besides friends, adolescent boys felt comfortable with doctors for discussing growing up issues. It might be because of the scientific explanation they received from the doctors which satisfied their queries appropriately. It can be noted that the responses (Figure. 5.1) on the basis of type of schools did not show much variation.

Knowledge and Perception of Adolescent Boys on Masturbation

Boys from government and private schools were asked to tell about the option which described the masturbation appropriately. On masturbation various myths and misconceptions prevail which included that it leads to dysfunction and deformity of sexual organs, it is a dirty/messy act etc.

The finding shows that very small number of respondents (from both government and private schools) considered masturbation as a natural practice. 17.5 per cent from government schools did not know about the masturbation while 40 per cent from private schools replied that they did not know about the same. Rest of the respondents considered that it was an unnatural practice. Age-wise data reflects that the respondents of 12-16 age group were more vulnerable as a large number of respondents had misconception that masturbation leads to dysfunction and deformity in sexual organs.

Feelings when Experienced Nocturnal Emission

Many of the adolescent boys may experience nocturnal emission/night fall (wet dreams). Formation and discharge of mature sperms can occur during adolescence and manifests as nocturnal emission. It signifies reproductive maturity for an adolescent boy. Respondents were asked to give information on whether they have experienced nocturnal emission/night fall in yes or no response and what were their feelings towards the same.

Data shows that the significant percentage of students (21.25 and 31.25

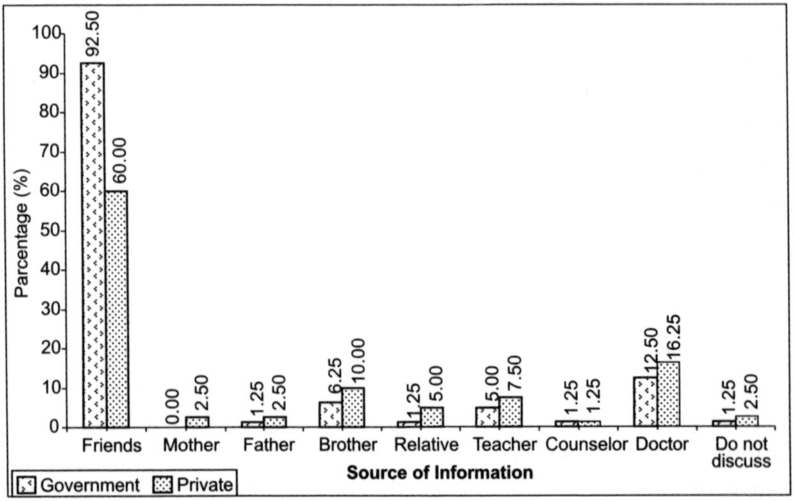

N= 80 (each type of school)

Figure 5.2: Source of Information on Nocturnal Emission and Type of School

from government and private schools respectively) became disturbed when they experienced nocturnal emission.

Source of Information on Nocturnal Emission

Adolescent boys were asked to tell about the source of information they accessed for the information on nocturnal emission. Friends, father, mother, brother, relative, teacher, counselor, doctor, and do not discuss were considered as sources of information on physiological changes. For each source of information, data have been collected from the 160 respondents (80 girls each from government and private school). Each respondent could give more than one response as this was a multiple response question. Only the affirmative responses for each source of information on physiological changes were considered in the Figure 5.2.

Overall analysis of the data reveals that the respondents considered friends as the most reliable source of information followed by the doctor, brother, and teacher to discuss on nocturnal emission. There was not much variation in the preference of the students according to the type of school.

Process of Growing up in Girls

Physical changes during adolescence are normal biological process. Like adolescent boys, girls also experience the rapid physical changes. They are sensitive towards these rapid changes and at times get affected by them psychologically in the absence of information and knowledge about these changes.

Level of Awareness on Physiological Changes Among Girls

The physiological changes among adolescent girls includes rapid gain in height and weight, growth of hairs in under arms, growth of hairs in pubic parts, white discharge from private parts, change in voice, development of breast, and onset of menstrual period. The level of awareness of the adolescent girls was examined on the above mentioned physical changes at three point scale, i.e., fully aware, partially aware, and not aware. Respondents' (girls) responses on level of awareness on the physiological changes were cross tabulated with their class and type of school.

Above analysis of the findings reflects that that a small percentage of students (girls) were fully aware, more than half of the respondents were partially aware on the physiological changes. It can be observed that a significant percentage of students were not at all aware (25 and 13.75 from government and private schools respectively). A considerable percentage of the respondents (partially aware or not aware) were vulnerable as wrong ideas can lead to confusion. Class-wise data shows that there was not much difference in the level of awareness on physiological changes among adolescents of secondary and senior secondary classes in both types of schools. The analysis of findings also reveals that there was not much variation in the level of awareness on physiological changes among government and private schools students.

Source of Information on Physiological Changes Experienced by Girls

The respondents (girls) were asked about the sources of information they accessed to know about the physiological changes. Friends, siblings, mother, father, teacher, counselor, doctor, and do not discuss were considered as sources of information on physiological changes. For each source of information, data have been collected from the 160 respondents (80 girls each from government and private school). Each respondent could give more than one response as this was a multiple response question. Only the affirmative responses for each source of information on physiological changes were considered.

The analysis of findings reveals that girls considered friends and mother as the most reliable source of information on physiological changes. It was noteworthy to observe that a considerable percentage of students did not discuss on physiological changes with anyone. School-wise analysis of findings did not reveal any significant variations.

Reactions of the Girls on the Physiological Changes Experienced

Girl students were asked to share about the reactions on physiological changes they have experienced whether they took it as natural process or became disturbed. Respondents' responses on the reaction on physiological changes experienced were cross tabulated with their type of school. The data have been further tabulated with the type of their family, i.e., joint, nuclear, and single parent family.

Data on type of family reveals that in the joint family 22 out of 32 and 17 out of 32 girls from government and private schools respectively considered physiological changes as a natural process. In the nuclear family 25 out of 43 and 32 out of 47 girls from government and private schools respectively became disturbed when experienced physiological changes.

Above analysis of findings reflect that a large percentage of girls became disturbed when they experienced physiological changes in both government and private schools. A significant number of girls belonged to joint family considered physiological changes as natural process than in the nuclear family. Many of the respondents shared that in joint family, they have multiple sources to obtain information as compared to nuclear family. School-wise analysis of findings did not show much variation.

Level of Awareness on Menstrual Period

Respondents (girls) were asked about the options describing menstrual period whether it was a sign of fertility or shedding of dirty blood. The data on options describing menstrual period was examined with the level of awareness – fully, partially, and not aware.

It can be observed that a significant number of respondents (33 and 30 from government and private schools respectively) responded that they were fully aware and described menstrual period as a process of shedding dirty blood. Hence they were more vulnerable as they felt that they have the right information although this was partial information. Responses on the basis of type of school did not show much variation (Table 5.1).

Table 5.1: Responses of the Girls About the Reactions on the Physiological Changes Experienced

Reactions	*Type of School*							
	Government				*Private*			
	Type of Family			*Total*	*Type of Family*			*Total*
	Joint	*Nuclear*	*Single Parent*		*Joint*	*Nuclear*	*Single Parent*	
Natural Process	22	18	2	42 (52.50%)	17	15	1	33 (41.25%)
Became Disturbed	10	25	3	38 (47.50%)	15	32	—	47 (58.75%)
Total	32 (40.00%)	43 (53.75%)	5 (6.25%)	80 (100.00%)	32 (40.00%)	47 (58.75%)	1 (1.25%)	80 (100.00%)

Source of Information Accessed before Starting of Menstrual Period

Onset of menstruation is a physiological process but myths and misconception are associated with it, and hygiene during menstruation is the most important concern. Students (girls) were asked whether they have accessed any source of information before starting of menstrual period. Mother, sister, cousin, friend, teacher, internet, T.V./radio books/newspaper, and do not discuss were considered as sources of information accessed before starting of menstrual period. For each source of information, data have been collected from the 160 respondents (80 girls each from government and private schools). Each respondent could give more than one response as this was a multiple response question. Only the affirmative responses for each source of information were considered.

From the findings it can be analysed that the mother, sister, friends and teacher were most approachable for the adolescent girls for obtaining information on menstrual period before the onset. No respondent has accessed internet as a source of information on menstrual period before the onset in both type of schools (government and private). A considerable number of students did not access any source of information.

Knowledge and Perception on Pregnancy

Teenage pregnancy has far reaching consequence in terms of adolescents' development, fertility rate and reproductive health. It also curtails education and alters their choice of careers. Early child bearing pose risk to both infants and mother. If girls who are not fully developed become pregnant, they can experience damage to their reproductive tracts, delayed or obstructed labour, rupture in the birth canal and increased risks of maternal mortality. Also teenage parents lack experience, skills and resources needed to raise their children.

In the previous section, on the process of growing up, the data of boys and girls have been examined separately in two sub-sections (process of growing up in boys, and process of growing up in girls). From this section onwards data of 320 students were collectively examined, i.e., 160 students (80 girls and 80 boys) from each stratum (government and private schools).

Knowledge and Perception on Pregnancy

Students' perception was assessed on whether they were aware of the process of pregnancy, i.e., by the union of sperms and ovum takes place, boy closely hugs/kisses a girl, and do not know. The respondents' perception on pregnancy was examined with the type of their school and further cross tabulated with their gender.

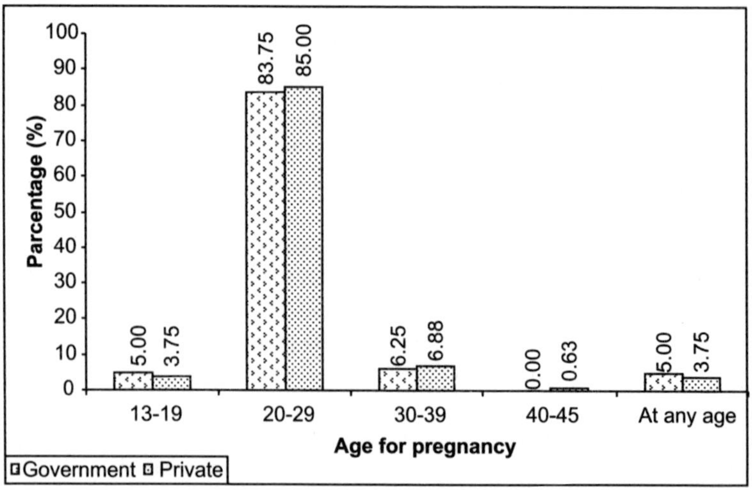

N = 160 (from each type of school)

Figure 5.3: Knowledge and Perception of the Respondents on the Right Age of Pregnancy

The findings reveal that a large percentage of students (36.26 and 41.26 from government and private schools) were not at all aware of the reason for pregnancy. A significant number of respondents cited that pregnancy occurs when a boy closely hugs /kisses a girl or either directly said that they did not know.

Knowledge and Perception of the Respondents on the Right Age of having Pregnancy

The data from 2001 census indicates that many of the girls married under the age of 15 years become mothers in the country. Teenage pregnancy causes many social, economical and health problems with the adolescents. The respondents' were asked about the right age of having pregnancy. The responses have been further categorized according to the type of school.

The data reflects that majority of the students from both government and private schools perceived that the right age of having pregnancy was 20-29 years. Nevertheless the disturbing fact was that there were a few respondents who perceived that the right age for having pregnancy was 13-19 years. The age group of 13-19 years for having pregnancy comes under the category of teenage pregnancy.

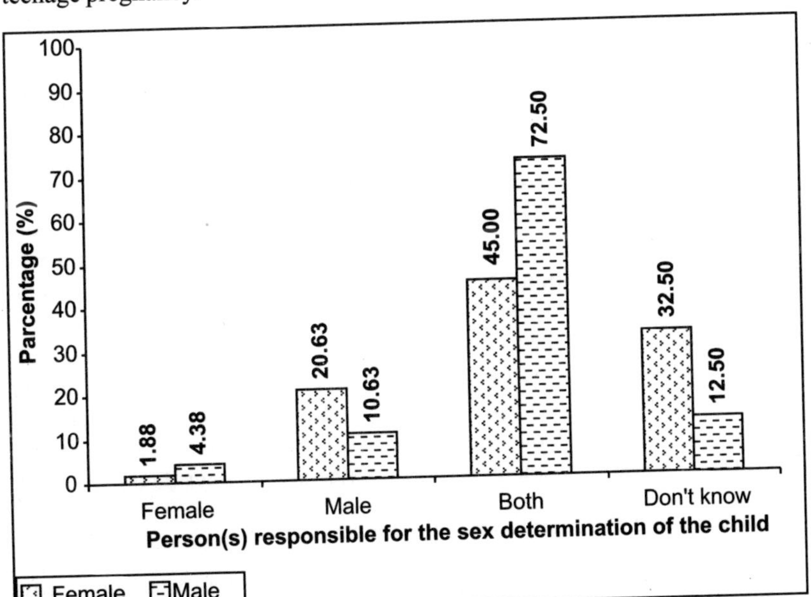

N= 160 (from each gender)

Figure 5.4: Knowledge and Perception of the Respondents on the Person Responsible for the Sex Determination of the Child

Person Responsible for the Sex Determination of the Child

Sex determination of a child depends on the X and Y chromosomes. The male has XY chromosomes while the female has XX chromosomes. Since the male has XY chromosomes, the sperm can contain either X or Y chromosome. If the egg which can only have X chromosome is fertilized by a sperm containing Y chromosome, baby boy is conceived. And if the egg is fertilized by a sperm with X chromosome a baby girl is conceived. Thus the baby's sex is determined by the male and not by the female parent. In this section respondents' were asked to tell about the person responsible for sex determination of a child.

The data clearly depicts that a significant percentage of the respondents (from both type of schools) have misconception that either both the parents or female parent was responsible for sex determination. A considerable percentage of students did not know who is responsible for sex determination of a child. Data reveals that a very less number of the students, i.e., 9, 7, 13, 21 from the IX, X, XI, XII respectively were aware about the fact that the male was responsible for the sex determination of the child. Although, there is a detailed explanation on the sex determination of a child in the Science Textbook of class Xth, NCERT, Delhi.

Source of Information on Pregnancy related Issues

The respondents were asked about the source of information they accessed to know about the pregnancy related issues. Mother, father, siblings, friends, teacher, internet, T.V./radio, books/newspaper, and do not receive were considered as sources accessed on pregnancy related information. For all source of information, data have been collected from the 320 respondents, i.e., 160 students (80 girls and 80 boys) from each government and private school. One respondent could give more than one response as this was a multiple response question. Only the affirmative responses for each source of information were considered.

Overall analysis of the data reveals that on pregnancy related issues friends were the most popular source of information among both boys and girls of government and private schools. Mother and siblings were considered as source of information by more girls than boys in both types of schools. Use of Internet and books/ newspaper is more popular among boys than girls.

Knowledge and Perception on Abortion

Unsafe abortions are a major source of reproductive mortality and morbidity. Many abortions are done illegally and often without adequate professional support, leading to serious reproductive morbidity. It has been observed by Jejeebhoy (1996) that adolescents constitute a sizeable proportion of the abortion seekers and many of the adolescent abortion seekers were unmarried girl.

Perception about the Conditions in which Abortion can be Done

Researches indicate that abortion is generally sought in the conditions when risks involved in carrying pregnancy for the health of the mother and foetus, pre-marital pregnancy, in case of female foetus, and also in case of unplanned pregnancy as a method of family planning. To examine the same, in the present research, respondents' perception was assessed about the conditions in which abortion can be done. The respondents were first asked whether they have heard about the abortion. All the respondents (320 students) replied that they had heard about the abortion. There were no significant variations in the responses of the respondents on the basis of the type of their school; hence the Figure 5.5 reflects the data of all the 320 respondents together.

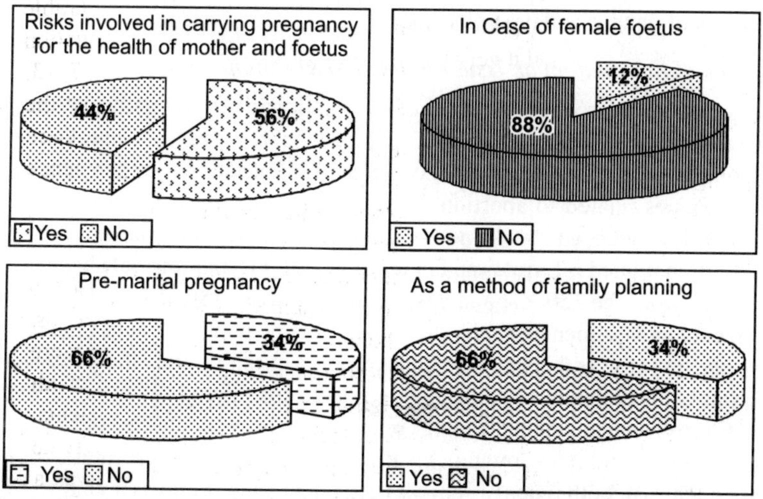

Figure 5.5: Perception about the Conditions in which Abortion can be done

Figure 5.5 reveals that in case when risks involved in carrying pregnancy for the health of the mother and foetus 56 per cent (179 out of 320) respondents agreed that abortion can be done.

In case of female foetus 12 per cent (38 out of 320) of the respondent perceived that abortion can be carried out.

34 per cent (109 out of 320) respondents were of the opinion that in case of pre-marital pregnancy also, abortion can be done.

There was related percentage of students (34%) who responded that the abortion can be sought as a method of family planning.

It can be observed that a large number of respondents had correct perception that abortion can be done in case when risks involved in carrying pregnancy for the health of the mother and foetus. However, a significant percentages of respondents perceived that abortion can be done in case of pre-marital pregnancy, In case of female foetus, or as a as a method of family planning.

Appropriate Person to Conduct Abortion

This sub-section deal with the perception of the adolescents on the appropriate person who could conduct abortion, i.e., a qualified doctor, or dai (traditional midwife). The analysis of the findings shows that a large percentage of the respondent considered doctor as an appropriate person to conduct abortion. Although, the significant percentage of the respondents had erroneous perception also that abortion can be performed by someone (dais) secretly. The data overall reflects that there was not much variation in the responses on the basis of gender and type of schools.

Sources of Information on Issues Related to Abortion

Adolescents access various sources of information in order to gain knowledge on reproductive health issues. Therefore, in the present research the respondents were asked to share the source of information they had accessed on the issues related to abortion. Mother, father, siblings, friends, teacher, internet, T.V./radio, and books/newspaper were considered as sources accessed on abortion related information. For all source of information, data have been collected from the 320 respondents, i.e., 160 students (80 girls and 80 boys) from each government and private school. One respondent could give more than one response as this was a multiple response question. Only the affirmative responses for each source of information were considered.

Overall analysis of the findings reveals that the responses on the basis of type of school did not show much variation. A significant percentage of the respondents (in both types of schools) considered T.V./radio as a vital source of information. Though, it has been observed that they considered I-Pill as a means of abortion, it implies partial awareness of the respondents. Gender-wise variations can be seen in the choice of source of information accessed by the respondents. Gender–wise data depicts that the friends and T.V./radio was popular among both boys and girls in both government and private schools to access information on issues related to abortion. Mother and siblings were more approachable to the girls than boys. Internet, books/newspaper, and teacher were accessed more by the boys than girls on issues related to abortion.

Knowledge and Perception on Contraceptives

Early pregnancy has a long term impact especially on the girl's life. It is important for both male and female to understand that both have an equal responsibility to avoid unwanted pregnancy. There are some of the contraceptive methods that can be used to prevent unwanted pregnancy and at the same time be protected from Sexually Transmitted Infections (STIs), including HIV/AIDS.

Level of Awareness on Contraceptives

Respondents' were asked to inform about whether they were aware of contraceptives, which can be used for safe sex. Those who were aware of the same were further asked to mention the name the contraceptives they were aware of.

All the respondents were either fully aware or partially aware, none of them reported that they were not aware of contraceptives which can be used for safe sex. They were also asked to mention the names of specific contraceptives. 132 out of 320 respondents were aware of condoms, 169 out of 320 respondents about pills, and 19 out of 320 respondents said that they were aware of both condoms and pills.

The data shows that none of the respondent reported that they were not aware on contraceptives. All of them were either partially or fully aware on contraceptives. In the previous section (knowledge and perception on abortion), it has already been observed that students considered I-Pill as a source for abortion also. While I-Pill is an emergency contraceptive and not a pill for abortion. Hence the respondents who claimed that they were fully aware about the contraceptives seem doubtful. Gender-wise data shows that more boys were fully aware than girls on contraceptives. The related data depicts that more girls were partially aware than boys on the awareness of contraceptives. A few of the respondents shared that they had pre-marital sexual relationship and were not aware of the condoms as a protective measures. They shared that they used the I-Pill (emergency contraceptive) after having the intercourse. That shows they were at risk of having STI/ HIV.

Sources of Information Related to Contraceptives

Reliable source of information on the sensitive issue like contraceptive is very much required. So that teenage/unwanted pregnancy can be prevented, as it has serious impact on the family, education, social life and health of the young mother and her child. Further, it was thought equally important to find out the source of information from where the respondents receive the information on contraceptives. T.V./radio, internet, posters, books, parents, peer group, teacher, counselor and doctor were considered as sources accessed on contraceptives related information. For all source of information, data have been collected from the 320 respondents, i.e., 160 students (80 girls and 80 boys) from each government and private school. One respondent could give more than one response as this was a multiple response question. Only the affirmative responses for each source of information were considered.

Overall analysis shows that there was not much variation on the basis of type of schools in accessing various sources of information related to contraceptives. Gender-wise data reflects that T.V./Radio, books and peer group were accessed by both girls and boys. Internet, posters, counselor and doctors were approached more by boys than girls.

Sexual Behaviour

This section is on the importance of socio cultural norms of sexual behaviour and healthy attitude towards the opposite sex: Abstinence till marriage, general social disapproval to pre-marital and extra-marital sexual relations, and respect for members of the opposite sex.

Perception Towards the Act of Sexual Intercourse

Respondents' perception was examined towards the act of sexual intercourse. Whether they consider sexual intercourse right only after marriage, only when mature enough, or when involved in love affair.

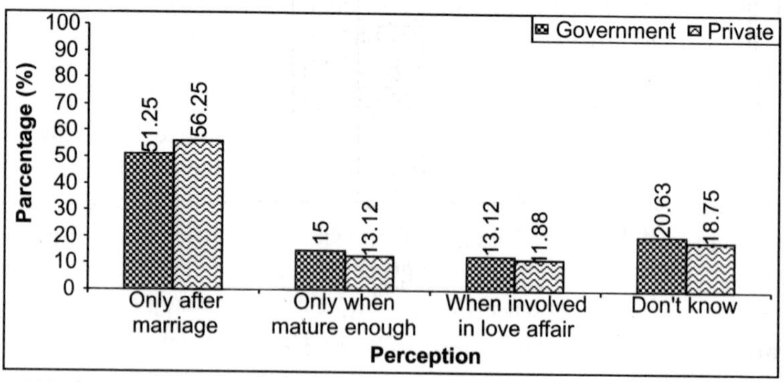

N = 160 (from each type of school)

Figure 5.6: Respondent's Perception towards the Act of Sexual Intercourse

Above findings show that a significant percentage of the respondents perceived that sexual intercourse was right when involved in love affair and nearly 20 per cent of the respondents from both type of schools did not know about the sexual intercourse.

Perception Towards Pre-marital Sexual Relationships

The pre-marital sexual relationship is believed to be a contentious as some consider it is permissible, others feel it is a taboo and should not take place before the nuptial bond is tied. Respondents' perception was also examined on the same components and further cross tabulated with the type of school.

There was not much variation in the responses of the respondents on the basis of the type of schools. When one say that pre-marital sexual relationship was permissible and normal as part of growth, it implies that the person should be well informed of the consequences or mature enough to take the informed decisions. A few of the respondents revealed that they were having pre-marital sexual relationship. At the same time they shared that they were not aware of the contraceptives much. Analysis of the above finding reveals that the respondents who were having pre-marital sexual relationship and were not aware of contraceptives were at risks of unplanned pregnancy, abortion, RTI/STI, and HIV infection.

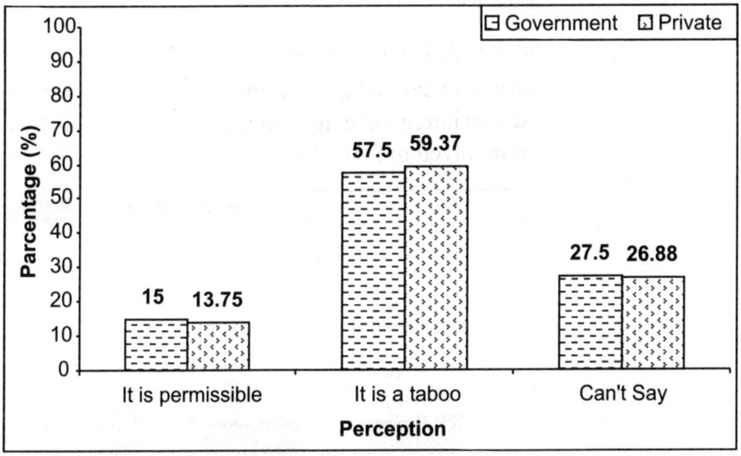

N= 160 (from each type of school)

Figure 5.7: Respondent's Perception towards Pre-Marital Sexual Relationships

Sexual abuse/Harassment

Abuse can be physical, sexual, emotional or verbal. Sexual abuse includes any situation in which a person (male/female) is being used for someone's sexual gratification, ranging from hands- on abuse, such as fondling or exposing to disturbing sexual material.

Act of Sexual Abuse Respondents' have Heard

Students were asked whether they heard about the sexual abuse/harassment. 288 out of 320 students heard about sexual abuse/harassment and 32 had never heard. School-wise data reflects that 146 and 142 students from the government and private schools respectively had heard about the sexual abuse/ harassment.

In Figure 5.8, for the each category of the act of sexual abuse, data have been collected from the 160 respondents from each type of schools

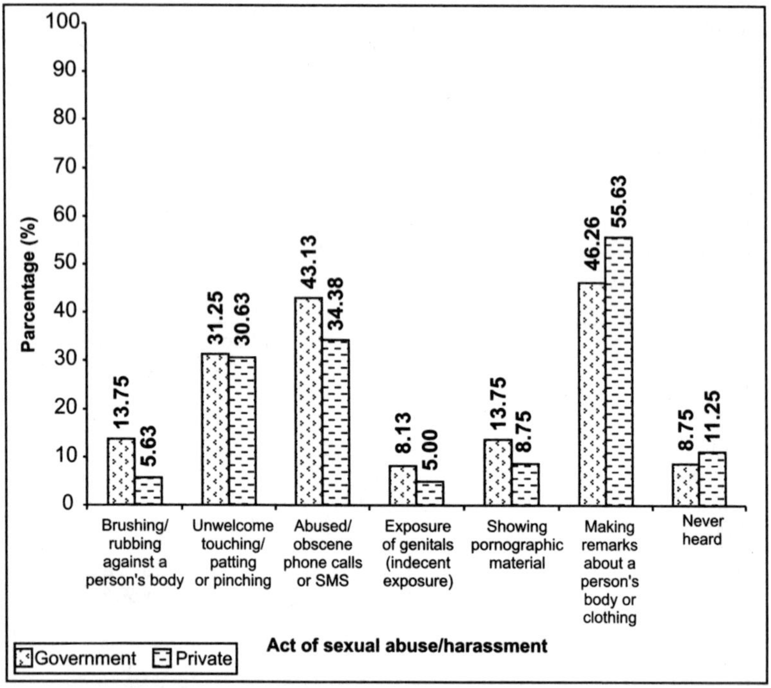

N= 160 (from each type of school)

Figure 5.8: Responses on the Act of Sexual Abuse Respondent's have heard

(government and private). Only affirmative responses for each act of sexual abuse were considered.

Overall analysis of the data reflects that a large percentage of the respondents had heard about one or the other form of the act of sexual abuse in both types of schools. It was significant to note that a considerable number of girls shared that they had been sexually abused by the close relative or the neighbor. They also disclosed that they felt very bad about the incidents and not able to confide to anyone.

Measures can be taken to Prevent Sexual Abuse/Harassment

Often adolescents are not aware of the ways of handling the situation of abuse. There are various measures through which the sexual abuse can be prevented but in the present study we have restricted it to only three measures, i.e., decent appearance and dressing, report to family members, and imparting self-defence training among adolescence. Decent appearance and dressing was taken as a measure because the available literature reflected that it is one of the measures to prevent the sexual abuse.

Data shows that 47.5 per cent of the male respondents considered that sexual abuse could be prevented through imparting self defence training among adolescents. 23.75 per cent felt that one should report to family members and 15.63 per cent replied that decent appearance and dressing was required to prevent sexual abuse.

Data reflects that 60.63 per cent of the female respondents also had the same perception that imparting self defence training among adolescents could prevent sexual abuse. 21.88 considered that it could be prevented through reporting to family members. 13.75 per cent felt that decent appearance and dressing could prevent sexual abuse.

It can be observed that both male and female respondents had similar views on measures to prevent sexual abuse. A significant percentage of respondents revealed that they did not know the measures to prevent sexual abuse, hence they were vulnerable. Self defence training was considered as a significant measure to prevent sexual abuse by both male and female respondents.

Knowledge and Perception about Sexually Transmitted Infections (STIS)

All those infections that are communicated through sexual contact with infected partners are known as sexually transmitted infections (STIs).

Knowledge about Sexually Transmitted Infections (STIs)

Sexually Transmitted Infections (STIs) can be treated (except HIV) if timely recognized (diagnosed) and actions are taken to consult qualified doctors. Respondents were asked whether they have heard about the STIs and know the symptoms of the STIs. 185 out 320 respondents had heard about STIs and 135 out 320 respondents had never heard about the same. In that also, 104 respondents replied that they knew the symptoms of STIs and 216 respondents did not know the symptoms.

Data reflects that in the government schools 10 per cent respondents recognized itching/reddening in the genital region a symptom of STIs. 8.13 per cent replied that genital ulcers/sores were symptom of STIs, followed by burning pain during urination (5%), lower abdominal pain (3.13%), and unusual genital discharge (3.13%). Majority of the respondents (70.63%) were not aware of the symptoms of sexually transmitted infections (STIs).

Lower abdominal pain was cited as a symptom of sexually transmitted infection by the 9.38 per cent of the respondents from private schools. Equal percentage of the respondents (9.38%) cited Itching/reddening in the genital region as a symptom of STIs. 8.13 per cent of the respondents considered genital ulcers/sores a symptom of STIs, followed by burning pain during urination (4.38%), unusual genital discharge (4.38%). 64.38 per cent of the respondents did not know about the symptoms of STIs.

Above findings show that a large percentage of the respondents did not know the symptoms of sexually transmitted infections (STIs). Not much variation had been seen school-wise and gender-wise.

Knowledge and Perception about HIV/AIDS

AIDS is caused due to Human Immunodeficiency Virus (HIV). It has emerged as an epidemic all over the world and it is infecting and affecting large sections of society and especially the adolescents. Adolescents are believed to belong to a group at risk of HIV. In spite of the fact that knowledge and awareness can prevent HIV, young people's access to information, skills, services and support regarding HIV is alarmingly low.

Knowledge and Perception about Various issues related to HIV/AIDS

It is very important to make adolescents aware of how a person can contribute in spread of HIV by simply reducing one's own vulnerability to the infection by increasing his/her own knowledge as well as learning some life skills. Respondents were asked whether they heard about the HIV/AIDS. 290 out of 320 respondents replied that they had heard about the HIV/AIDS. 30 respondents did not hear about the HIV/AIDS.

Table 5.2: Knowledge and Perception about Various Issues Related to HIV/AIDS

Perception	*Type of School*							
	Government			*Total*	*Private*			*Total*
	Yes	*No*	*Do not know*		*Yes*	*No*	*Do not know*	
HIV/AIDS spreads from an infected blood transfusion	134	15	11	160 (100.00%)	120	14	26	160 (100.00%)
HIV/AIDS spreads through using infected syringe	134	15	11	160 (100.00%)	121	12	27	160 (100.00%)
HIV/AIDS can be transmitted through pregnant woman to her unborn child	134	10	16	160 (100.00%)	115	19	26	160 (100.00%)
HIV/AIDS spreads through unprotected sexual contacts with infected partner	136	9	15	160 (100.00%)	123	14	23	160 (100.00%)
HIV/AIDS spreads by sharing a meal	29	114	17	160 (100.00%)	31	102	27	160 (100.00%)
HIV/AIDS spreads from a mosquito bite	49	91	20	160 (100.00%)	45	81	34	160 (100.00%)

Overall analysis of data reflected that a large number of respondents were aware of the various means of spread of HIV/AIDS. Though above findings depicts that a significant number of respondents were either did not know, or had wrong information on the means of spread of HIV/AIDS.

Substance Abuse: Myths and Misconception related to Substance Abuse

Substance abuse refers to the overindulgence in and dependence on a stimulant, depressant, chemical substance, herb (plant); leading to affect that is detrimental to the individual's physical health or mental health, or the welfare of others. Addiction of substance abuse is a compulsion to repeat behaviour regardless of its consequences.

Perception of Adolescents on Various issues related to Substance Abuse

There are various myths and misconceptions exist with regard to substance abuse. Respondents were examined on various issue related to substance abuse. These included; drug sharpens thinking and concentration, drug addiction can be cured by medical and psychological treatment, and self determination is necessary to overcome drug addiction. For each category, data had been collected from 320 respondents, i.e., 160 students each from government and private school (Fig. 5.9).

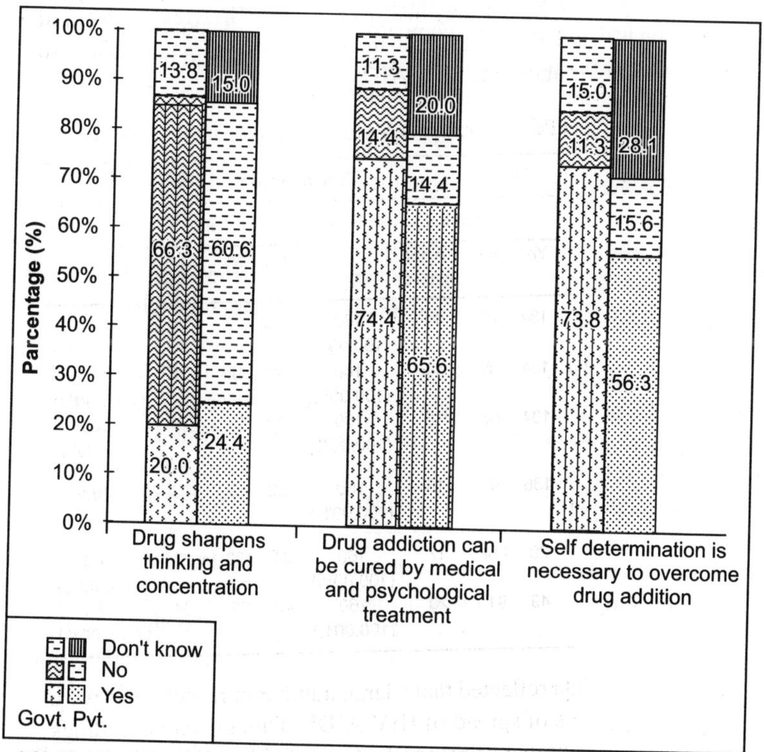

N= 160 (from each type of school)

Figure 5.9: Knowledge and Perception of Students on Various Issues related to Substance Abuse

The Figure 5.9 reflects that 66.3 per cent of the respondents from the government schools agreed that drugs did not sharpen thinking and concentration. 20 per cents considered that it sharpens the thinking and 13.8 per cent did not know about the same. 74.4 per cent of the respondents perceived that drug addiction can be cured by medical and psychological treatment. 73.8 per cent felt that self determination is required to overcome drug addiction.

In the private schools 60.6 per cent respondents felt that drugs did not sharpen thinking and concentration. 24.4 per cent considered that it sharpens the thinking and 15 per cent did not know about the same. 65.6 per cent of the respondents perceived that drug addiction can be cured by medical and psychological treatment. 56.3 per cent felt that self determination is required to overcome drug addiction.

From above findings it can be analysed that a large percentage of respondents were aware that drugs did not sharpen thinking and concentration, drug addiction can be cured by medical and psychological treatment, and self determination is required to overcome drug addiction. It could also be observed that a significant percentage of the respondents either did not know and had wrong idea about the various issues related to substance abuse.

Substance not Considered as Drug Abuse

Respondents were asked to tell about the options which were not considered drug abuse.

For the each category of the substances not considered as drug abuse, data have been collected from the 160 respondents from each type of schools (government and private). Only affirmative responses for each category were considered.

Findings show that 61.88 per cent respondents from the government schools did not consider disprin as a drug abuse. 38.75 per cent of the respondents shared that pan with tobacco was not a drug. Data reflects that the considerable percentages of the respondents did not consider bhang (19.38%), gutaka (16.25%), tobacco (16.25%), and alcohol (8.75%) as a drug abuse.

Data reflects that from the private schools 48.75 per cent of the respondents did not consider disprin as drug abuse. 30.63 per cent responded that pan with out tobacco was not a drug abuse. Like the data from the government school considerable percentages of the respondent did not consider tobacco (22.5%), bhang (16.25%), gutaka (10.63%), and alcohol (10.63%) as a drug abuse.

It was evident from the above findings that a significant percentage of the respondents did not consider tobacco, bhang, gutaka, and alcohol as drug abuse. Hence, it was apparent that they were not aware that these substances were also come in the category of drug abuse.

Conclusion

In this chapter knowledge and perception of adolescent students was assessed on various reproductive health issues and it was found that significant number of students from both government and private schools were partially aware. The partial awareness of the adolescent students implies that the knowledge and information they have on physiologically issues was not always correct. The incorrect information is likely to lead to misinterpretation and misuse. The findings reflected that there is no significant differences found in the knowledge and perception on reproductive health issues among adolescent students on the basis of type of school (government and private school), and classes (secondary and senior secondary classes). Various sources of information were accessed by the adolescents on reproductive health issues. Gender-wise variations can be seen in the choice of source of information accessed by the adolescent students. Friends and T.V./radio was popular among both boys and girls. Mother and siblings were more approachable to the girls than boys. Internet, books/newspaper, and teacher were accessed more by the boys than girls.

6

Need of Imparting Reproductive Heath Education: Opinion

Despite the fact that the school equips adolescents with the knowledge, skills and inculcates in them positive attitude to face the rigors of the world, the role of family is crucial in the total personality development. Parents are primary educators and play a critical role in shaping the individuality of the adolescents. In India the issues related to reproductive health have been carefully kept out of the education process within the family. It is felt essential for the parents to appreciate the urgency of imparting reproductive health education to their growing up children. Parents have to recognize that adolescence is a period of rapid growth and development. They should respect the identity and the right to privacy of adolescents. The behaviour of parents has a powerful influence on adolescents. Parents can very effectively influence the process of growth of their adolescents if they, establish a close relationship with them. The adolescents need to be assured that they can talk with their parents on all the issues including those relating to their process of growing up. Parents are particularly expected to share the knowledge about the physical, emotional and social growth and developmental changes taking place during puberty with their growing up adolescents. It may not be possible, and even necessary for every parent to go into the details. But it is certainly expected of them that they should provide at least the essential knowledge to their adolescent children at the appropriate time.

It is very well noted that for any educational innovation the teacher occupies a pivotal role. Most of the elements of reproductive health education are sensitive, delicate and value laden. Interaction with adolescent students on these elements can be effective only when a holistic approach is adopted. The entire environment is to be made congenial to impart knowledge in these elements to adolescent students. The first and foremost requirement for the teachers is to be convinced about not only the need but also the urgency of imparting reproductive health education to adolescent students. So far, we have been teaching adolescent students almost everything about human body and mind except the process of growing up during adolescence. Once convinced, teachers have to equip themselves well for imparting reproductive health education to students effectively. It is very natural that teachers, like any other groups of society are influenced by the cultural setting and have inhibitions regarding sex related matters. They have to be helped in getting rid of such inhibitions. Teachers will have to be resourceful so that they can handle sensitive topics with ease and care. It is also necessary, sometimes, for teachers to perform the functions of counselor. Since teachers are trusted by the students they can conveniently gain the confidence of students and ably act as counselors. The advice given by teachers is more acceptable to students. It is however, extremely important for teachers to be non-judgmental so that students are treated by them as individuals who need their compassion and care.

It is agreed upon that adolescence is a period of rapid change both physical and psychological. During this phase adolescents need right kind of education related to their growing up issues. Parents and teachers have a vital role in imparting reproductive health education. In this chapter the author has examined the opinion of the parents, teachers and adolescents on imparting reproductive health education among adolescents. Parents whose children were studying between class IX-XII in a co-educational government or private school In the National Capital Territory of Delhi and teachers teaching any of the classes between class IX-XII of a co-educational government or private school In the National Capital Territory of Delhi were selected for the study. Adolescent students both male and female studying between classes IX- XII in a co- educational government or private school in the National Capital Territory of Delhi were selected for the study. Sample comprised of 10 teachers and 10 parents from each (four) selected school thus the total sample size is 40 teachers and 40 parents and total sample size of students is 320. It has been seen in the data gathered that the responses of parents, teachers and adolescents of government and private schools do not show much variations. Hence, the research findings are presented under the themes and further sub-categorized in two or three sub-themes namely Parents' Opinion, Teachers' Opinion and adolescents' opinion.

Reproductive Health Needs of the Adolescents

Adolescence is a period of growth and development from the onset of puberty to maturity (Bancroft and Reinisch, 1990). Adolescence is a critical phase during which significant personality reorganization occurs. The suddenness and rapid pace, with which the changes take place in the body and mind of adolescents, generate a number of problems and special reproductive needs which adolescents find difficult to understand on their own.

Parents' Opinion

It is significant to note that all the respondents (40/40) accepted that the adolescents have certain reproductive health needs Parents reflected on the fact that adolescents should be aware of personal hygiene, changes they are undergoing in adolescence, balanced diet and right guidance on various issues. It was also observed in the statements given by parents that adolescents are not getting information and those who received it may not be correct all the time. Parents were also concerned about the subject that they can not deal with all the issues of reproductive health. Specifically they pointed out that:

- Adolescents need to know about personal hygiene, guidance on health problems, they eat junk food so making them understand about balanced diet, deal with their anxiety they feel because of physical changes and besides this need is of moral education and healthy parent child relationship.
- Knowledge and guidance on biological changes and related information about menstrual cycle.
- Right guidance at right time. (6 out of 40 respondents)
- As they grow because of the changes they become frustrated, feel irritated on little issues, they behave negatively with parents. So there is a need to guide them to take care of their psychological needs.
- Adolescents get knowledge from their mother but not complete as mothers are also not much aware. Boys should also know as the time changing. (3/40 respondents)
- They should be aware of right and wrong.

It was noted that parents talked about the rights of adolescents, decision making was also given importance. Parents also highlighted the fact that there is a need to keep an eye on adolescents' activities by saying that:

- Adolescents need special care. There is a need to handle their issues carefully like how they look at mirror, what they watch in T.V., what knowledge/information they are receiving from the T.V., their peer group activities, what they are talking over phone/issues of their conversation with friends, their body language/gestures. (4/40)
- Parents should attend regular Parent Teacher Meeting (P.T.M.) so that they can watch the activities of adolescents not only related to studies but the behaviour of the child with the teachers, girls/ boys, address each and every report given by the teacher. (4/40)
- There is a gap between the age of parents and children, adolescents need some privacy. They have some existence in world, right to say

yes or no, we should respect them, and they should be well informed on reproductive health issues.

- Right direction and guidance with regards to their decision making on reproductive health matters should be given importance. (8/40)

Teachers' Opinion

Findings of the study revealed that the teachers' also agreed on the fact that adolescents have certain reproductive health needs with regards to their holistic growth and development. There was only one teacher who felt that there is no specific reproductive health need of adolescents for their growth and development, and adolescents did not require any special attention. While other respondents (39/40) of the study articulated that adolescents reproductive health needs ranged from good health, right information, quality literature on reproductive health issues, friendly environment, family support and care, healthy peer interaction etc... The respondents of the study said that:

- Parents have a vital role in socialization- adolescents need parental affection, interaction, and time. They definitely need guidance on good and bad touch. (5/40)
- Nutrition is a vital need, adolescents eat more fast food, they like coke (cold drink) instead of milk. They are not physically strong. Adolescents need good health, environment, diet, and most important is literature. (12/40)
- Adolescents experience physiological changes so need to give knowledge according to that age. They feel hesitated and insulted if something happen wrong in the class. "agar menses class me start ho jaate hain aur dress par stain lag jaate hain, toh girls bahut hi insulted feel karti hain" (if the menses starts in the class and got stains on the uniform, girls feel insulted). There is a need to tell them in advance by parents and teachers.
- Adolescents are in confused state of mind. They want to be treated as adults, whereas, it is required that they learn to adjust with their age. They are in the phase where they need to adjust with their growing age. They have identity and role confusion. (9/40)
- Education and guidance need to be imparted to both boys and girls on the physical changes they are undergoing.
- Most of them are anemic, so need to know about nutrition, need for balanced diet, health related problems, and counseling.

Teachers emphasized on the point that media hampers the growth of the adolescents. They watch T.V. a lot which affects their growth. They know each and everything which they should not, it ultimately hampers their growth. Some teachers also added that a component of moral education may be added in the reproductive health education module. They said:

- Adolescents' cultural development is needed. There is a need to give them proper socialization, moral education. If we (teachers) will speak on it (reproductive health issues), they start laughing so, need a school counselor.
- In government schools many of the students are from slums. During physical changes they use abusive language. They write and paint dirty messages on the walls "students school ke corridor, washroom me bahut he vulgar pictures banate hain" (Students draw vulgar pictures in the corridor and washroom of the school). If we hide things, their level of curiosity will get increased and it will affect their emotional, mental and educational development. Hence there is a need to give them some moral education too.
- They need to understand society and social relationships. As the adolescents are not knowledgeable so, need to tell them everything in proper detail. There is need to tell them with the help of examples, tell them about the reproductive health diseases.

With the words of caution teachers said that:

- There is need to give adolescents right information at right age and in right content. (5/40)

School's Responsibility for Holistic Growth and Development

Parents' Opinion

All the parents (40/40) opined that school has a responsibility to help and guide the students for their holistic growth and development. Parents conveyed that though it is a responsibility of school but teachers has so much to do. Besides this there are the parents who considered that parents and teachers have equal responsibility. Few parents felt that the parents have prime responsibility. The below statements given by the parents reflect their opinion:

- Teachers can make adolescents understand well, we (parents) can not. They follow the teacher as a role model. Students respect teacher more than parents and easily accept whatever teacher says. (4/40)
- Everything related to education, they are getting from school so it is good if this education should be given by them
- Maximum time students spend is in school but parents and teachers have equal responsibility. (2/40)
- Certain schools have taken the responsibility. They are providing the counseling but they are burdened with other assignments.
- School has a secondary responsibility. The family has a prime responsibility to help and guide their children. With girls it is a responsibility of mother and with boys its father. (3/40)

Peer Group role was emphasized and Media role was also discussed by parents. Some parents stressed on the duties of the teachers, and they feel even parents also need reproductive health education:

- School deals with the same age group children so, peer group discussions are healthy. The way of thinking becomes almost same as they get same answer of their queries. (7/40)
- Media is giving half information so they need complete and right information.
- School should give the right report of the students to parents, exact status of the behaviour - what the child is doing. Parent teacher interaction is needed. Parent should be aware of their rights to get complete information regarding the child's performance.
- It is good if school takes responsibility. Educate parents too on reproductive health issues. (10/40)

Teachers' Opinion

Two teachers were not in favour that school has responsibility to help and guide students for their growth and development. Some of the teachers were in favour to certain extent but not much, it was conveyed by the teachers that its one extra responsibility and they feel overburdened. Teachers cited that:

- No, it is not school's responsibility. Teachers already have so much to do. They learn on their own.
- Not much, everything is there in the books so no extra information is needed. Whatever is there in the syllabus is enough. If school sees something wrong then prevent the same.
- School has a great responsibility, but time constraints are there. We have continuous classes.Teacher has to deal with 40-50 students. Every teacher is over burdened to complete the syllabus. If some students need the help and guidance we provide otherwise we would not. (12/40)

Teachers stressed on the role of the parents and specifically mother. They felt that family has a primary responsibility. Media's role was also highlighted by the teachers:

- Teachers' responsibility is to certain level, Parents should be much more responsible. Every child has a different psychology some feel *"ohhhh kya bata rahe hein"*.
- Most important is mother's role. First its mother's responsibility, we are second educator. (5/40)
- Media is telling why we (teachers) cannot. (2/40)
- Media is playing a great role so, school's role is marginal. (2/40)

Most of the teachers were in favour (13/40) and cited that its teachers' responsibility but somehow they have not taken, teachers are role model, school has a great impact on adolescents etc.:

- To great extent- students are from poor family background, uneducated parents. So, teacher has a responsibility to help and guide them.
- Teachers play a vital role in motivating the students towards right direction. Adolescents consider teachers as role model. Adolescents can not speak to their parents, they can speak to teachers freely.
- Definitely school has a great impact on personality of the students. School can give reproductive health education in a balanced way. Students would not feel misguided or confused. Teachers and counselors should help and guide the students.
- Teachers' role is very important. There are contents on reproductive health education in Biology chapters which needs to explain with elaboration. Cite examples so that students get answer without asking the questions which will reduce their level of anxiety.

With a word of caution, teachers cited that:

- School should have proper environment, staff, facilities, and time. Special counselor should be there.
- It (reproductive health education) should be provided by using proper method of education.
- Teachers' role in moral education is very necessary. Through inculcating good moral values, the adolescents can be helped in distinguishing between 'right' and 'wrong'.

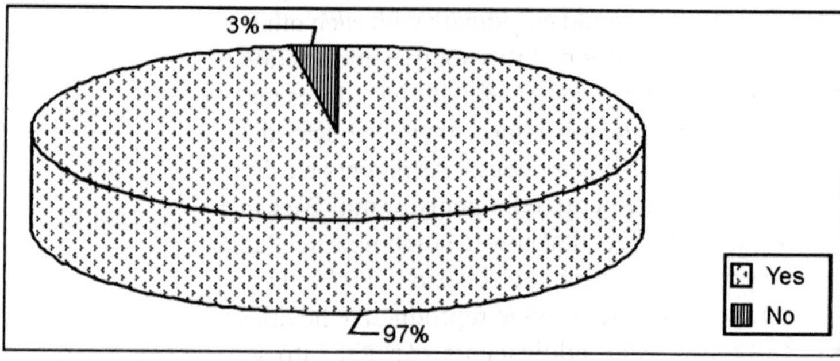

Figure 6.1: Opinion of Parents on the Necessity to Impart Reproductive Health Education in Schools (N=40)

Necessity to Impart Reproductive Health Education

Parents' Opinion

Parents were interviewed to know their opinion on the necessity to impart reproductive health education in schools for adolescents.

Figure 6.1 reflects that except one (3%) parent all were in favour of imparting reproductive health education in school. The reason cited was:

- It is not the responsibility of schools. The responsibility goes to the parents. It is good if school provides but it is not their responsibility. Primary responsibility is of the parents

Other parents opined that like other subjects reproductive health education should also be given by school teachers. Parents also mentioned that school is the best place because adolescents learn in a better way in their peer group. Few parents stressed on the point that school counselor or expert can take sessions and parents and teachers should be a part of the same. They also emphasized on the role of school, as messages from media some times are not appropriate. Parents cited that:

- Teachers teach students on various issues and it will be effective if they take the responsibility to teach and guide students on reproductive health issues.
- At certain age adolescents require reproductive health education. It is not necessary they get the same from family atmosphere. But school definitely can provide the same as the students are of same age group in the class and equally need the education on reproductive health issues.
- Some issues can not be discussed with the child by the parents. School can call counselor, psychologist for taking sessions. Both parents and teachers should coordinate with each other, understand that they have mutual responsibility to give information to the child.
- In contemporary scenario if the adolescents are not aware of reproductive health issues, they feel scared *"ek Hawwa si lagati hai"* (It seems like an issue). As parents we do not know the limit to tell them, whether to tell openly or not. We can not speak to them- a hesitation is there that how to communicate. Parents need not to speak on such issues because of respect *"aankho ki sharam honi chayiye"*. It is necessary to provide reproductive health education in schools.
- In today's time adolescents can get into wrong company. T.V. advertisement give generalized information so, they need to be made aware of right information at right age. What they watch through T.V., cinema, and internet, need right direction on that.

Teachers' Opinion

Teachers have a pivotal role in imparting reproductive health education to adolescents. Hence, the teachers were asked to give their opinion on the same. Teachers' responses on the same are reflected in the Figure 6.2.

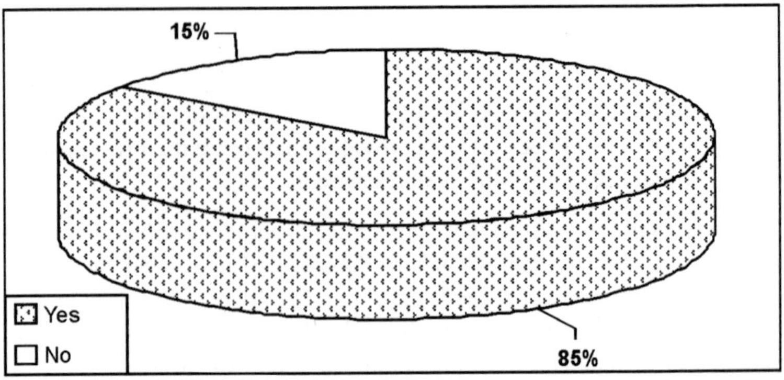

Figure 6.2: Opinion of Teachers on the Necessity to Impart Reproductive Health Education in Schools (N = 40)

It has been noted that six (15%) of the teachers do not think important to impart reproductive health education in schools. They cited different reasons like instead of providing reproductive health education in schools provide quality literature on it, students will misinterpret the information given by the teacher and promiscuity will get increased, they learn through their own experiences, the content is there in science books so no need to tell about it separately, statements of teachers are given below:

- No, do not give in co-education school. There is no comfortable environment, girls will feel shy, students will misinterpret, if they will get open and do experiment. If reproductive health education be given everything will get destroyed, *"Chingari ko hawwa doge toh aag to bhadkegi"*
- No it is not necessary. They learn through their own experiences. If we will become more open they could take liberty and do experiment for example, Condom- they could feel of experimenting. *"condom use karo, toh kya saare galat kam karo?"*. Tell them at right time, keep it as secret. Now T.V. advertisements telling about it openly, children are coming forward. We should tell them in limits.

The teachers who felt that it is necessary to impart reproductive health education, they opined that imparting reproductive health education help adolescents to get right information and they will not feel misguided or misinformed. Teachers also stressed on appointing a counselor for imparting reproductive health education. Some teachers were in favour that reproductive health education should be provided as like other subject or as a part of Science/ Home Science subject. Few teachers also said that school is best as there are same age group adolescents. Media has a vital role to play was realized by few teachers.

- Guidance is needed. For example, a student of sixth class in our school caught with a nude photograph from a newspaper. School has created an issue while it should have been taken casually. Such students belong to poor socio economic background where there is one room, parents are making love in front of them. There is an urgent need to impart reproductive health education in schools.
- Students have misconceptions so there is a need to deal with that. Knowledge is needed. Boys write abusive language at walls. So school should educate them for creating proper environment.
- Sometimes they commit some mistake. If they are aware, they will not do so. School can impart reproductive health education as one of the subject.
- There is a need to have counselors in the schools who could speak to adolescents comfortably without hesitation.
- There are chapters related to reproductive health in the syllabus. Each and every thing should be told to students. Its not a matter of *"shame or pride"*, should not feel awkward. So impart proper knowledge which will take them to the right direction.
- Adolescence is the age of physical and psychological changes, attraction towards opposite gender is very high for example, girls say *"boys toh chedenge hi"*. So they need guidance. Impact in the same age group is much better then dealing separately with adolescents.
- Today's generation has become mature at early age because of media influence so they need to know about precautions. For example, for unwanted pregnancy emergency pills so they need to know about its side effects. There is need to deal with their curiosity through proper education. Chapters dealing with reproductive health issues in books should be dealt very carefully and properly.

One of the teachers felt that it is a joint responsibility of both parents and teachers and commented that:

- Make the adolescents understand about themselves. Identity crisis is there, they are not open to their parents. One needs to understand them. Teachers and parents should give proper time to them and help them in decision making. Stress overloading is there, so we need to deal with that.

Adolescents' Opinion

Both boys and girls (N=320) from private and government schools were interviewed to know about their opinion on the necessity to impart reproductive health education in schools.

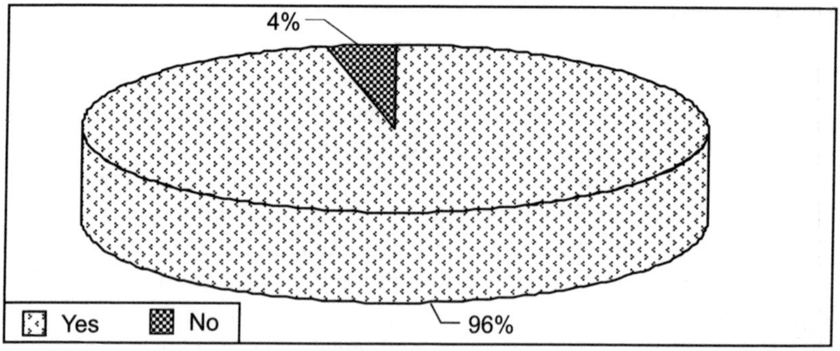

Figure 6.3: Opinion of the Adolescents on the Necessity to Impart Reproductive Health Education in Schools (N=320)

Figure 6.3 reflected that 308 students (96%) felt that it is necessary to impart reproductive health education while 12 students (4%) were not in favour. Students cited various reasons in support of their opinion like:

- Need to make the young generation aware about reproductive health Issues
- It helps adolescents to know the harmful effects of the unhealthy risky behaviour
- It will broaden our thinking and prevent us from teenage pregnancy, unprotected sex and RTI/STI/HIV/AIDS
- It will help in developing positive attitude towards reproductive health issues
- It will prevent adolescents from getting wrong information from other sources and prevent from committing mistakes. It helps in taking right decisions.
- One can not ask parents directly on each and every aspect of reproductive health issues

The students who do not feel the necessity to impart reproductive health education said that:

- Do not want to discuss as feel shy. It is a personal issue so need not to be discussed.
- There are many other elements such as T.V., internet, radio etc. by which a large number of people can get information

An Appropriate Class from which Reproductive Health Education Should be Started

Parents' Opinion

Parents were asked to give their opinion on the class from which reproductive health education can be imparted to the students. The responses received from parents were represented in the Figure 6.4.

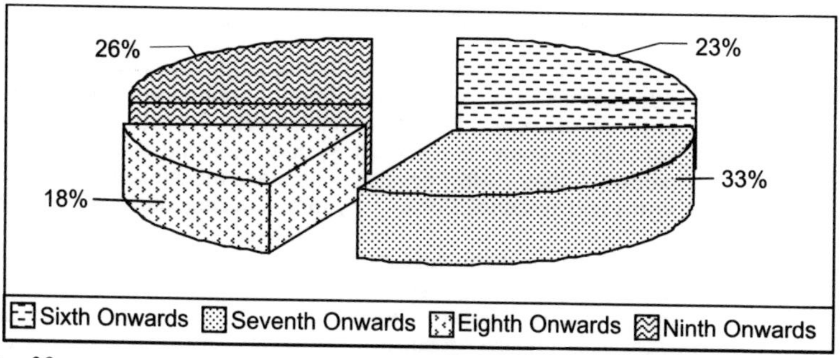

N = 39

Note: One of the parents' responses was not taken in this component as (s)he was against of imparting reproductive health education in school.

Figure 6.4: Opinion of Parents—An appropriate Class from which Reproductive Health Education should be Started (N = 39)

Teachers' Opinion

Similar to parents' findings the teachers also suggested that from sixth, eighth or ninth onwards reproductive heath education can be started. Their preferences can be seen in the Figure 6.5.

Parents and teachers cited various reasons for initiating reproductive health education among adolescents from one particular class. Their responses were categorized according to the class they have suggested for starting the reproductive health education (Table 6.1).

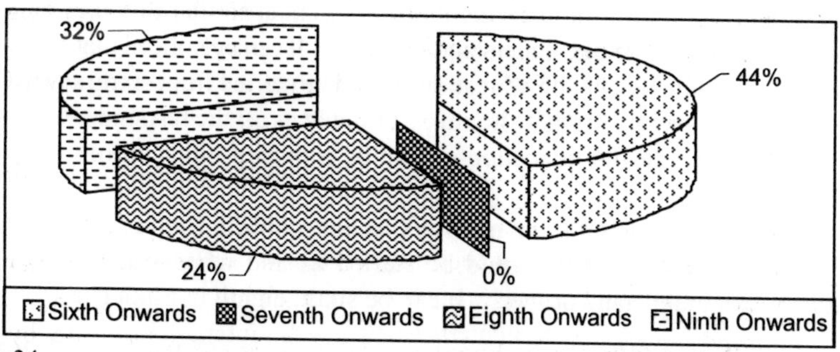

N=34

Note: Six of the respondents felt that it is not necessary to impart reproductive health education, hence their view on appropriate class for the same was not taken.

Figure 6.5: Opinion of Teachers - An Appropriate Class from which Reproductive Health Education should be Started (N = 34)

Table 6.1: Reasons for Initiating Reproductive Health Education among Adolescents from One Particular Class

S. No	*Class*	*Reasons cited by Parents*	*Reasons cited by Teachers*
1.	**Sixth**	Adolescents experience physical changes, they have curiosity to know. If not dealt properly they will develop myths and misconceptions.	Attain maturity and can understand about reproductive system. Entering in adolescents-girls starts menstruating and boys starts masturbating so need information.
2.	**Seventh**	They attain maturity and can understand well. They are not much aware hence need reproductive health education.	
3.	**Eighth**	They experience physical changes. They do experiments so need right kind of education. They should be aware of before the initiation of menstrual periods.	Reproductive developments starts from this age and changes are visible. Give them complete, proper age specific knowledge.
4.	**Ninth**	It is a puberty age and they experience changes so need knowledge. Need to initiate at this level and in eleventh-twelfth it should be in details.	Physical, mental, and social development start from this age. Knowingly or unknowingly they are observing things which enhance their curiosity to know about reproductive health issues. They are influence with peer group discussion. Need right education, else can be misleaded.

From above it can be seen that though parents have their own views on the class from which reproductive health education should be started, but reason behind a particular class mentioned is almost similar that they attain maturity, physical changes, understand well etc… It can be noticed that parents cited that reproductive health education should be started from sixth, seventh, eighth or ninth, but by ninth it should be initiated as all the respondents cited that reproductive health education should be provided either from ninth or before that.

Teachers also felt the same ways as the parents that education on reproductive health issues should be started as and when students attain maturity, can understand properly. It can be sixth, eighth or ninth class.

> It is seen from the findings that both parents and teachers felt that either from ninth or before that adolescents should be given reproductive health education.

Reproductive Health Issues to be Included in Reproductive Health Education

Parents' Opinion

Parents were interviewed to suggest the topics, which can be included in reproductive health education. The responses came from the respondents are reflected in the Figure 6.6.

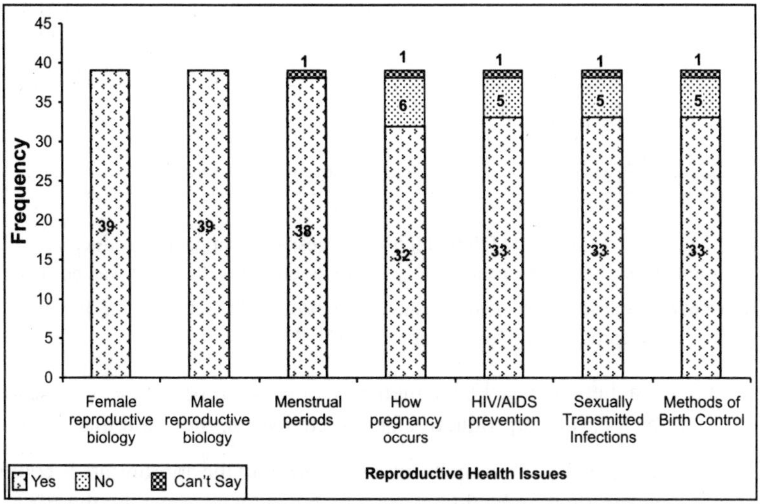

N=39

Note: one of the parents' responses was not taken in this component as (s)he was against of imparting reproductive health education in school.

Figure 6.6: Reproductive Health Issues Suggested by Parents to be Included in Reproductive Health Education (N=39)

Parents were also asked to tell about other topics/issues which they feel should be addressed in reproductive health education module. They specifically mentioned the following:

- Social values to both girls and boys like family adjustment/ family bonding/ parent- child relationship, gender sensitization
- Sexual harassment, role of media, highlight the role of parents
- Problems they can encounter related to sex relationships. In this age they have attraction towards opposite sex so need value education

Teachers' Opinion

There were various topics suggested by the teachers, which can be included in reproductive health education. The responses from the respondents are reflected in the Figure 6.7.

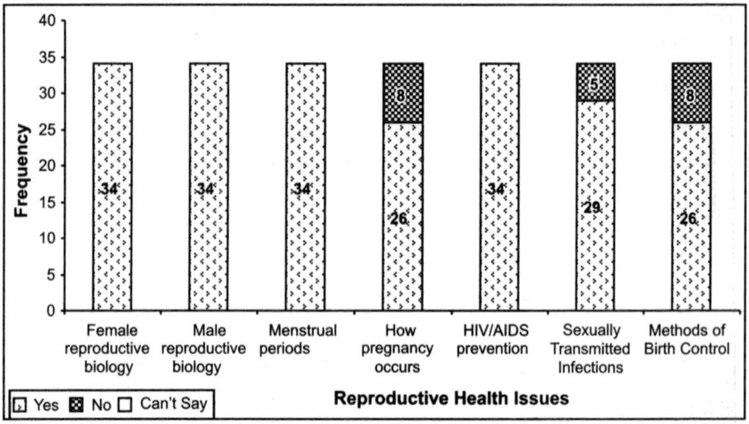

N=34

Note: Six of the respondents felt that it is not necessary to impart reproductive health education; hence their view on appropriate class for the same was not taken.

Figure 6.7: Reproductive Health Issues Suggested by Teachers to be Included in Reproductive Health Education (N=34)

When teachers were asked to mention some other topics they considered which can be a part of reproductive health education, they said that:

- Balanced diet, Telling the adolescents about the appropriate literature on reproductive health issues which can be accessed by them
- Provide moral education to prevent pregnancy and abortion.
- Need to conduct session on how to deal with mental and psychological stress. They are doing things repeatedly without knowing that what they are doing. It affects their social relationships and develops psychological disorders so, need counselor for counseling.
- Conduct session on how to do upbringing of the child during and after the delivery.
- Need to promote religious thoughts, moral values. Tell them about hazards, perspective, and reasons of providing reproductive health education. Adolescents have analytical mind so, must tell the reason of providing such education.

Adolescents' Opinion

Adolescents were interviewed to suggest the topics, which can be included in reproductive health education. The responses received from the respondents are reflected in the Figure 6.8.

It can be seen that respondents wanted that all the topics mentioned in the Figure 6.8 should be included as part of reproductive health education.

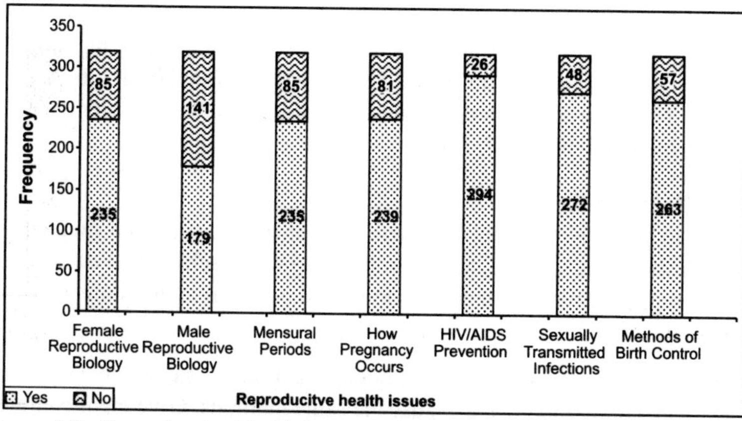

Figure 6.8: Reproductive Health Issues as Suggested by Adolescents to be Included in Reproductive Health Education (N = 320)

Appropriate Methods for Discussing Reproductive Health Issues

Parents' Opinion

Most of the parents have opined that one single method for imparting reproductive health education is not effective. All the methods are equally important. They may be use as per the requirement and needs of different group of adolescents. Discussion with adolescents on reproductive health issues was most preferred method of teaching in parents' opinion. It has also been believed by parents that discussion should be used with other methods. Some parents preferred problem solving method in combination with other methods. The same opinion was reflected in the following statements made by the respondents:

- Discussion is very effective in a way, students can ask questions. Encourage them to ask questions. For example, one of the parents shared that during her school days a boy in her class was slapped by the biology teacher on asking a question about male reproductive organs. She felt that it was an inappropriate behaviour of the teacher.
- Lecture and discussion method will also prove effective. Do not make it a *"Hawwa"* (issue), take it easy in a natural way. If someone is feeling disturbed, we can provide counseling
- Use live experiences, discuss case studies. Talk to adolescents about good or bad touch.
- Use visual methods, documentary movies can be screened and then have discussions on it—it should be interesting, informative and should not be disgraceful (cheap).

- Provide counseling then discussion with each student about his/her problem. In other methods, can have experience sharing sessions like interaction with People Living with HIV/AIDS (P.L.H.A.).
- There is a need to hold discussion first and after that problem- solving method will be effective

Teachers' Opinion

Similar to parents' opinion, Teachers also opined that all the methods of teaching should be utilized in the combination with each other. Few teachers felt that reproductive health education should be given in the same way as in other subjects:

- No need to use special methods. Teach in the same way as you are teaching other subjects, use the same methods. Give them complete knowledge, no need to adopt different method. They should not feel that something different/ special is being taught. Encourage them to ask questions and discuss so that hesitation can be removed

Discussion was considered most effective way to communicate with adolescents in combination with other methods. Teachers also opined that interactive educational activities can be conducted along with other methods. Counseling, problem solving and discussing with each students are some of the ways teachers felt can be used together. Teachers stressed on the fact that only lecture will not be effective. Below are the statements expressed by the teachers:

- Only use of Lecture method would not work, rest of the methods are good.
- Discussion is must, identify points and then discuss them. Conduct interactive education activities, share life experiences as students take interest in that. Use electronic media.
- General Discussion followed by providing individual attention to each student about his/her problems and then provide appropriate counseling.
- Lecture method is good followed by Discussion. Slide show and screen documentary movies and showing reproduction on animals not on human beings. For e.g., discovery channel- they show animals.
- Counseling is very important. Besides this problem solving method can be used and discussing with each student about his/her problem. Case studies from real life experiences can also be taken up as an example.

In addition teachers also talked about the methods which can be very effective like:

- Teachers can ask students to write their problems and give to the teacher, later the teacher will address the issues.
- Initiate a seminar so that they will learn besides the class room. Counseling is must. Session on reproductive health should be made compulsory in each school at least two periods every week with each class
- Discuss on curiosity. If someone is going wrong then use inquiry method. Show slides and CD and then ask questions. Use of audio-visual aids is very effective.

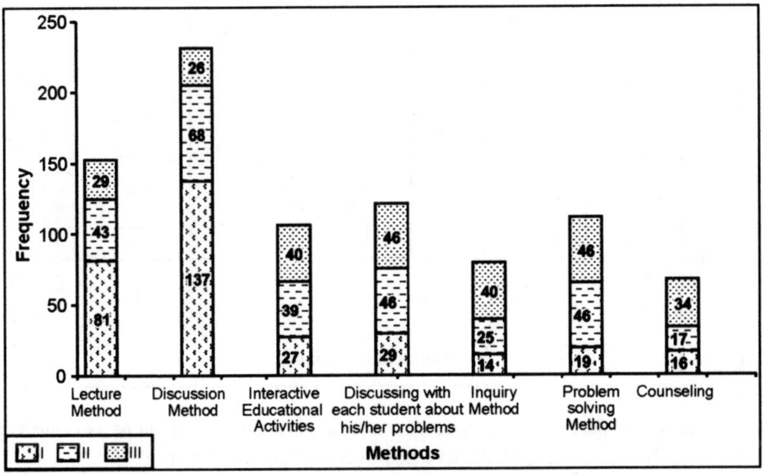

* The total number of responses is more than the total number of respondents because of multiple responses

Figure 6.9: Opinion of the Adolescents on Appropriate Method for Learning the Reproductive Health Issues (N = 320)

Adolescents' Opinion

Students were asked to give priority (I, II, and III) to the appropriate method for learning on reproductive health issues. Figure 6.9 reflected various priority mentioned by the students.

Students preferred the discussion method as the most appropriate and then lecture method. They cited that lecture method should be followed by some other method also like discussion, interactive activities, slide presentation or case examples etc...

Appropriate Source of Information

Parents, teachers and adolescent students were asked to give their opinion on the appropriate source of information from where the adolescents can learn on reproductive health issues.

Parents' Opinion

The below given Figure (6.10) reflects the parents' opinion on the appropriate source of information for adolescents to learn about reproductive health issues.

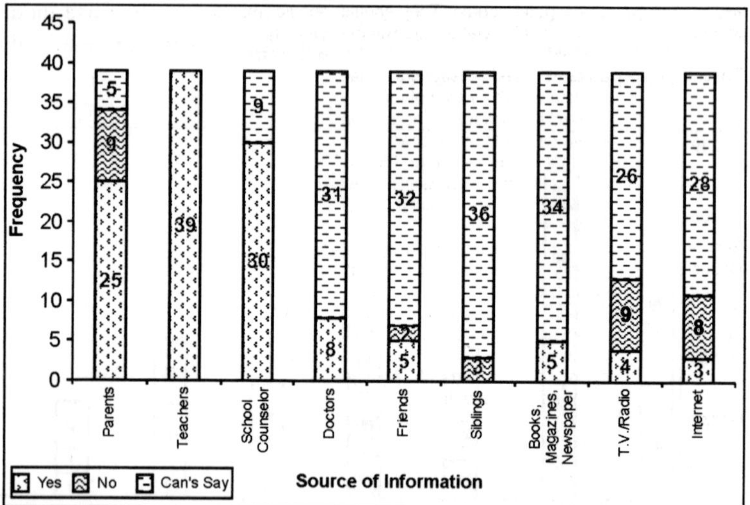

N=39

Note: one of the parents' responses was not taken in this component as (s)he was against imparting reproductive health education in school.

Figure 6.10: Opinion of Parents on the Appropriate Source of Information for Adolescents to Learn about Reproductive Health Issues (N=39)

Parents cited various reasons in support of their opinion which are presented in the Table 6.2.

Teachers' Opinion

The Figure 6.11 reflects the teachers' opinion on the influential source of information for adolescents to learn about reproductive health issues.

Teachers cited various reason in support of their opinion which are presented in the table 6.3

One of the teachers also highlighted that some special department can be formed specifically for this purpose. The respondent added that:

- Some special department should be there in the school to speak to adolescents on reproductive health issues.

Table 6.2: Appropriate Source of Information Suggested by Parents to Impart Reproductive Health Education and the Reasons Cited in Support of their Opinion

S. No.	*Source of Information*	*Reasons in support cited by the parents*	*Reasons cited by parents who do not support*
1.	Parents- Mother is cited as most important	As they spend maximum time with children It is a good source. They should have friendly relationship without hesitation.	Parents can not explain properly as they have a limited knowledge. They should maintain a distance because there are certain moral values, so it is difficult for them.
2.	Teachers	Student and teachers can discuss its two - way method. Students believe more on whatever is told by teacher. Teachers can be more friendly with students. Students feel comfortable in sharing with teachers.	
3.	School Counselor	Only the skilled person should provide reproductive health education. School counselors should compulsorily be appointed in all the schools. It is a very good source, counseling is essential.	
4.	Doctor	Doctors can make students understand very well with scientific knowledge. They explain very nicely because of the clarity of concepts.	
5.	Friends	Friends as they influence each other to a large extent	Friends have limited knowledge. Friends are immature
6.	Siblings		Siblings also have limited knowledge They might have misconception
7.	Books/ Magazines/ Newspaper	Should be selective as per the curriculum, every class has different curriculum It is good to certain extent.	
8.	T.V./Radio	T.V. information is enough Lots of campaign comes so it is good. Like condom so it is a best medium.	One would not have a choice to choose the programs according to the age-group. Adolescents need guidance through one to one interaction. Media is not appropriate as its one-way method. E.g. I Pill, an emergency contraceptive pills, advertisement would not tell after effects of the pills. It should be banned.
9.	Internet	Internet is a major source- we can give informative mails to students through NGOs or institutions related with these issues. E-mail Id can be collected with the help of parents and teachers. It gives enough information	Through internet they can access wrong information which could mislead. After enough maturity, they can use internet for such informations. If school will give sufficient information, no need to approach other methods

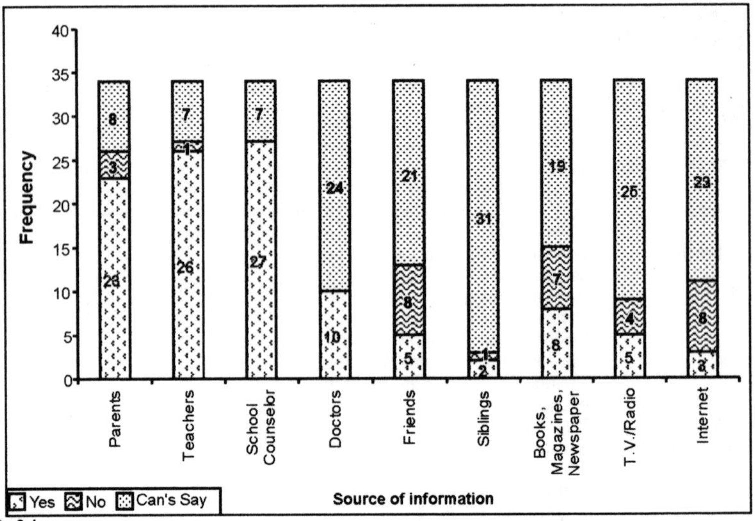

N=34

Note: Six of the respondents felt that it is not necessary to impart reproductive health education; hence their view on appropriate class for the same was not taken.

Figure 6.11: Opinion of Teachers on the Appropriate Source of Information for Adolescents to Learn about Reproductive Health Issues (N = 34)

Adolescents' Opinion

Figure 6.12 reveals the opinion of adolescents on the appropriate source of information to learn about reproductive health issues.

Adolescent students reflected that the teachers would be most appropriate source of information followed by doctors, social workers, counselors, NGO representatives and nurses.

Reaction, when Adolescents ask Information

Parents and teachers were interviewed to know how they react when adolescents ask information on reproductive health issues.

Parents' Opinion

Most of the parents (31) felt that they will avoid talking to the adolescents if they ask information on reproductive health issues or else they will tell a little bit. This is very much reflected in the statements given by them:

- I try to avoid (*Tal Matol karna)* because of our relationship I do not want to get close to my children- a distance should be maintained in order to maintain a respect. When they get married and they ask something, I will definitely tell them.

Table 6.3: Appropriate Source of Information Suggested by Teachers to Impart Reproductive Health Education and the Reasons Cited in Support of their Opinion

S. No.	*Source of Information*	*Reasons Cited by the Teachers in support*	*Reasons cited by the teachers who do not support*
1.	Parents	Parents and children are in direct contact They have an important role in socialization of their children.	They might feel hesitant Would not have time so they can not
2.	Teachers	Teachers can be a significant source in providing information to adolescents as they have great impact on students' life. Sometimes adolescents would not listen to parents, but listen carefully to teachers. They are the role model to students.	It is difficult for teachers. They have to be tough and strict, whereas for providing this type of education s/he needs to be polite.
3.	School Counselor	Because adolescents are not in regular touch with them so they can share their feelings openly. Yes it is a must at least one counselors should be appointed in each school. Counselor is essential as they can understand the problems of students well and have more time as compare to teacher.	
4.	Doctor	Doctors are better as they can explain well on biological issues They can guide on the study material which students can access.	
5.	Friends	Most interactions happen in peer group "*Dost ki baat pathar ki lakeer hai*" So promote peer group education.	Friends share a lot but how much is correct, can not say.
6.	Siblings	Elder ones can give	As like friends they will give incomplete knowledge.
7.	Books/ Magazines/ Newspaper	Books are very effective source of information and both print and electronic media can be used for disseminating information among adolescents.	Some considered that the information from books can be misinterpreted, misunderstood by adolescents
8.	T.V./Radio	Should telecast programmes on particular day and time which we can show to girls and boys. For e.g., Programme like Pragya, Love guru. It is more effective.	The information received from T.V./ radio can be misused by the adolescents.
9.	Internet	Lots of information is available.	Information can be misinterpreted, students misuse it.

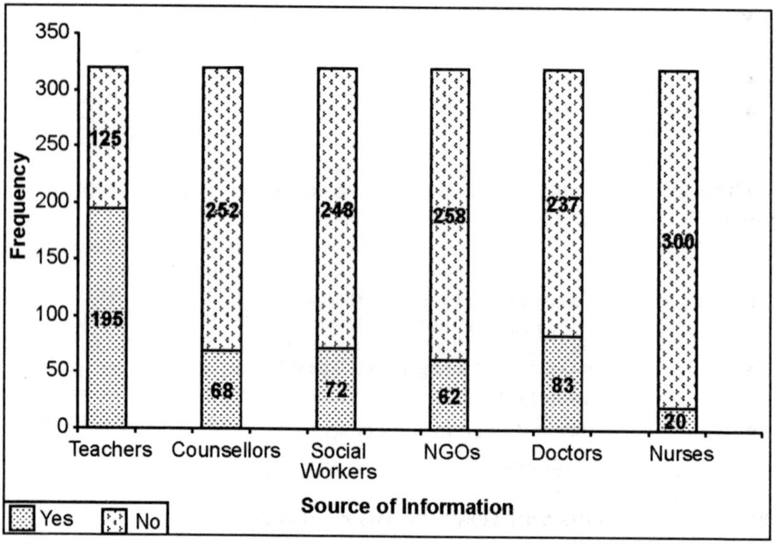

N=320

Figure 6.12: Opinion of the Adolescents on the Appropriate Source of Information to Learn about the Reproductive Health Issues (N = 320)

- I will not be able to clarify easily. If it is urgently needed, I will try my level best.

There were parents (8) who responded that they will definitely address the issues ask by the adolescents. They cited that:

- If she asks something which is not appropriate to tell her at that time, I will explain her some information according to her level and then assure her that the more information will be given at a right time. I feel if I leave her queries unaddressed, she will explore through other sources which could lead to misconception.
- As a good parent, I make him/her understand/explain/clarify doubts. I will guide with a positive attitude.

Teachers' Opinion

It is to be noted that most of the teachers felt that they will explain to the adolescents on reproductive health issues, if they ask. They expressed that it is necessary to deal with adolescents queries, if left unaddressed it will create curiosity and they can approach wrong source. They strongly felt that teachers should explain each and every detail. They supported their views by saying that:

- An adolescent will ask whenever s/he will face problem so, it is better to tell them.

- I will appreciate and motivate. It is better if s/he asking me. I will clear his/her doubts according to the age and level of understanding.
- I will tell them about positive thinking and give information.
- I will listen and then explain. As some students are not much aware and can commit something serious

There were few teachers who wanted to address the issues of adolescents but expressed that they can speak with specific gender, hesitation is there, etc... They cited that:

- It is difficult to express my views. If it is a boy I might tell in separate but if it is a girl I might not.
- I will react according to age group. Depends if the child is very young (small), I will not tell.
- Such issues are not open in society so some hesitation will be there, I will try to explain

Need to Make Parents and Teachers Aware of their Role

Parents' Opinion

Only two parents felt that there is no need to make parents and teachers aware of their role as an educator and the need to be effective communicators to adolescents. They cited that:

- No, parents are busy would not have time.
- Not needed for parents and teachers, as they are already trained.

Rest of the parents (37) strongly agreed that parents and teachers required to become an effective communicators to adolescents. They stressed that there is need to conduct training session with parents and teachers so that that they can effectively deal with their adolescents on reproductive health issues. Parents also stressed on the point that parents and teachers should meet during PTM (Parent Teacher Meeting) and discuss on the matters related to reproductive health education. They conveyed that:

- Yes, it is definitely needed. The special department can hold session for parents and teachers. If parents and teachers are well informed they could help that department in disseminating information to students. Coordination between parents, teachers and special department is required to impart effective education among students.
- School should hold sessions for parents. We will definitely go for our child in school ""*Agar school hame bulayega, hum turrant jayenge*". School should be active to ensure parents' involvement in school activities.

- Yes, it is needed. PTM (Parent Teacher Meeting) can train teachers and parents together. Adolescence is a sensitive age, need to handle properly. Adolescents are mentally confused so need counseling.

Teachers' Opinion

Teachers considered that that there is need to make parents and teachers aware of their role as an educator and there is need to be effective communicators to adolescents. Although they felt that teachers are already trained so they would not require any training, parents might need that some. Most of the teachers shared that there is need to make parents and teachers aware of their role as an effective educator to the adolescents. They conveyed that communication skills are necessary, need to organize meetings and seminars, need to know how to respond and talk to adolescents. They quoted that:

- Teachers are already educated, they have studied all things in B. Ed.
- Yes, Yuva programme has the provision for this. So teachers are already getting the training.
- Yes, coming to their level. A platform is needed to tell them the importance of reproductive health education in fact needs to tell both the parents.
- Yes, there are certain topics, even we are not aware. If a small child is asking something- how to answer for e.g., pregnancy.

Concluding Remarks by Parents and Teachers

Parents' Responses

Parents were asked if they have any comment or suggestion on the issue of reproductive health education. All the parents gave their opinion and suggestions. They commented that reproductive health education should be given to both boys and girls, parents and teachers should help the students in decision making. One of the parents cited that:

- Reproductive health education should be given without creating much hype; we should accept its importance. For example if a girl has an affair with a boy, parents and teachers should take it casually, explain to both the adolescents about each and every aspect so that they can think in a healthy way and can make proper choices for their decision. Parents and teachers should respect the adolescents' individuality, decisions, and activities. They should be watchful but in a way that child should not feel *" meri Jasoosi ho rahi hai"*. We should have some equal rules for children of both gender like when to come back home, should have a fair attitude for both the gender.

Most of the parents felt that schools should make reproductive health education mandatory. They said school is one place where students get same knowledge so the scope of misinterpretation is reduced. They also added that school should involve the parents too. They suggested that Parent Teacher Meeting (PTM) could be one platform where these issues can be discussed:

- Parents have different knowledge on reproductive health issues so they tell concept according to their knowledge with their children. Students discuss all the information received from parents and various sources in their peer group and they get confused and conceive wrong concepts. Teachers impart same knowledge to whole class so scope is not there to develop misconception.
- School should initiate to provide the reproductive health education to the students as the teachers are educated enough to explain properly. School should take initiative and involve the parents.
- If the school will provide the reproductive health education, it will help the parents. Children will not face any problem in schools, for e.g., teenage pregnancy and frequent abortions can be reduced. It is certainly for the betterment of the children, they have lots of myths and misconceptions.
- There is a need of interaction between parents and teachers on this issue. Like PTM, Parents and teachers can meet regularly and strengthen the programme on reproductive health education.

Parents were also of the opinion that school counselors should be appointed to provide reproductive health education and stressed that parents and teachers should also be involved in the same. They added that:

- Reproductive health education should be given as other subjects are taught in the school. Counselor should be appointed to take sessions in classes in a healthy environment.
- Doctors or some specialists should be invited sometimes to conduct special session for parents and teachers too. They should cite examples, conduct case discussions, discuss situation and how to handle those situations. These kind of workshops should become a regular feature in all the schools.

Parents also stressed on the point that reproductive health education should be given gradually and appropriately in a culture sensitive manner,

- It is necessary to provide reproductive health education but according to the prevailing cultural norms in the society. Adolescents will definitely take information on reproductive health issues whether from proper or improper sources so, it is better to give them information but gradually and appropriately like breakfast at morning, lunch at afternoon and dinner at night. First of all educate parents and teachers

- Right education at right age and give information slowly according to their age and class.
- Should give reproductive health education in a healthy manner. Give the information cautiously so that they would not take it negatively and misuse, and misinterpret. This age is sensitive so, needs right education at right time.

Parents raised a very important issue that the children from low socio-economic family, who are staying in one room need the reproductive health education, media's crucial role was also emphasized by parents. They also added that component on moral values also required such education:

- Family atmosphere should be balanced, for e.g., in slums there is only one room, everything is happening in front of children. T.V. shows showing everything in detail which is not good. We should deal with it.
- Teachers' should regularly interact with the students. But students do experiment so, it has negative impact too. Should stress on moral values-control and limits should be there.

Teachers' Responses

Almost all the teachers commented and suggested on the issues of reproductive health education. Most of them said that there should be school counselor for providing such education.

- There is a need to appoint counselors in schools. Teachers are already overburdened. Students should be made aware that physical changes are natural biological process. They should not feel shy and discuss with ease with their parents. Adolescents should make themselves safe. Even if abuse takes place, they usually do not share with their parents. They get pregnant and abort the same with the help of their boyfriends without disclosing it to their parents. I-Pill is creating a major blunder. There should be a ban on T. V. advertisement like I-Pill. Earlier there was a fear of abortion among unmarried youth but now they have I-Pill. If you do a survey you will find maximum sell of I-pill is amongst adolescent unmarried girls. Students should know safety measures and after effects. If a student commits some mistakes, do not make him realize as s/he has done some sin. Ask them to learn from mistakes. Do not compel them to commit suicide. Parents' education is very essential.

School counselor should give this education as teachers have less time available. Students will also feel comfortable with them.

- During reproductive health education, students should be informed about dangerous diseases, unwanted pregnancy, about simple medicines. There is a need to appoint special counselors in all schools. Special needs of adolescents should be addressed at the school level. Proper funding is needed to run programmes related to reproductive health education.
- There is a need to have school counselor so that they can deal with students' feelings in each and every way. Teachers can not share on all the issues.

Like parents, teachers also stressed on the point that a component on moral values should be incorporated with reproductive health education programme. They also added that it should be culture sensitive and given gradually in an appropriate way:

- Moral values should be given to students. They need to be told how to maintain healthy relationships.
- Start slowly and provide reproductive health education according to age. Gradually they can be imparted in depth reproductive health education.
- Stress should be laid on good manners as *"manners make a man"*. They should be taught how to behave in society.
- If we give them education on reproductive health issues, first we need to give education on moral values, social norms, social restrictions, and prevailing norms of Indian society. Purpose of reproductive health education should be made clear to the adolescents. We should tell them about right and wrong, advantages and disadvantages of reproductive health education. Simultaneously tell them about Indian culture.

Media's significant role is cited by the teachers and suggested to have provision of telephonic counseling:

- Media's role is very important. There is a need of availability of telephonic counseling.

Teachers also suggested to name the programme as *'healthy living'*. They were also of the opinion that a regular monitoring is required. They cited that the motive of the reproductive health education is being disregarded by the people hence need to take action. Teachers cited that:

- The motive of this education is getting ignored by the people. They feel it is for the pleasure while it is not so. It is to prevent society from dangerous diseases. There is a need to correct the viewpoint of teachers and parents
- Name it as health issues for boys and girls or healthy living. Do not emphasize much on other issues just address it. Encourage students to ask questions. Put up a question box in schools and address later.
- There is a need to do monitoring and evaluation of the reproductive health education given to the students that how they are utilizing the information. Bring modification accordingly. It should not misguide them.

Teachers suggested that there is a need to work in coordination with parents, teachers and government. Teachers were also of the view that students should not be stopped to learn about reproductive health issues and cited that

- Teachers should not feel hesitant about reproductive health education. "It should flow as river flows, if we try to stop students learning on reproductive health education, it will not stop so, better to give a direction to the flow from the starting point itself".
- Not only parents and teachers but government should assume responsibility. Like advertisements on HIV/AIDS, create awareness on reproductive health needs of the adolescents. There is a need to make adolescents responsible citizen of society.

Conclusion

This chapter highlighted that almost all the parents, teachers and adolescents opined that adolescents have physical, psychological and social needs associated with reproductive health issues which should be addressed properly. Most important is the right guidance at right time by the trained and skilled persons on all the growing up issues of the adolescents. Parents, teachers and adolescents have also added that a component on moral values should be incorporated with reproductive health education programme. It should be culture sensitive and given gradually in an appropriate way. Parents, teachers and adolescents emphasized on the need to appoint school counselor. They stressed on the fact that the parents and teachers also have accountability.

7

Way Forward

Adolescents are considered as the 'generation of hope', and play a vital role in the health status of any country. Their behaviors, attitudes, and beliefs are shaping the societies of the future. Thus, it is imperative to promote healthy practices during adolescence and to prepare them for the transition to adulthood. Previous chapters reflected that the adolescents are often reluctant to ask parents and teachers for details about reproductive health issues, fearing that questions might raise suspicions of illicit activity. Parents and teachers, on the other hand, may wish to discuss reproductive health issues with adolescents but are not equipped to do so. The end result is that adolescents are left in the dark and lack access to reliable information. If unaddressed, this situation can put the health and well-being of adolescents at risk. Schools are a safe place for adolescents to learn about reproductive health matters in age-appropriate ways. While information and education should be adjusted to the developmental level of the adolescents, reproductive health education must reach adolescents before sexual initial. Adolescents can benefit from continuing reproductive health education. The following recommendations would help in imparting productive health education in an effective way.

Recommendations by the Author on the Basis of Findings of the Data Collected from the Adolescent Students

In this sub section recommendations were derived by the author on the basis of findings of the data collected from the adolescent students (both boys and girls). It was recommended that:

- The adolescents required a right kind of education at right time.
- The reproductive health education should be started from the secondary classes onwards. It can even be started before that.
- Peer education needs to be promoted. Peer education is effective as peers considered to be more reliable.

- Sessions on reproductive health may be organized regularly in schools by experts.
- Adolescents are more vulnerable as they feel that they have the right information, it may be partial information. There is a need to build up on this information responsibly hence, it requires education and support from parents, teachers, and school administration.
- There is a need to provide training to parents too so that they can help the adolescents to obtain information on reproductive health issues.
- There is a need to create awareness among adolescents about:
  - ➢ male and female reproductive biology
  - ➢ conditions and consequences of teenage pregnancy and its impact on family, education and health of the mother
  - ➢ scientific knowledge, facts and figures related to contraceptives
  - ➢ different forms of sexual abuse and different ways to handle abuse.
  - ➢ knowledge, awareness and treatment of Sexually Transmitted Infections (STIs)
  - ➢ knowledge, awareness on HIV/ADIS (learn life skill to protect them from risky behaviour so that they can prevent themselves from HIV infection).
  - ➢ nastiest outcome of drug abuse.

Recommendations Given by the Parents on Imparting Reproductive Health Education to Adolescents

The research aimed to devise interventions to impart reproductive health education in an effective way, the recommendations given by the respondents (parents) themselves were found worth considering which are presented below:

- Reproductive health education should be given to both boys and girls. It should be given to adolescents gradually and appropriately in a culture sensitive manner.
- Parents and teachers should help the adolescents in decision making. Parents and teachers should respect the adolescents' individuality, decisions, and activities.
- There is a need of interaction between parents and teachers on reproductive health issues. Parent Teacher Meeting (PTM) could be one platform where these issues can be discussed to strengthen the programme on reproductive health education
- School counselors should be appointed to provide reproductive health education.
- Experts can be invited by the schools to conduct sessions on reproductive health education. Parents and teachers should also be involved.

- There is also a need to introduce component on moral values in reproductive health education.

Recommendations Given by the Teachers on Imparting Reproductive Health Education to Adolescents

Almost all the teachers suggested on the issues of reproductive health education. Most of them said that there should be school counselor for providing reproductive health education. They recommended that:

- There is a need to appoint school counselor in all schools. Proper funding is required to run programmes related to reproductive health education.
- Purpose of imparting reproductive health education should be made clear to the adolescent students. There is a need to tell them about right and wrong, advantages and disadvantages of reproductive health education. Simultaneously tell them about the Indian culture.
- Regular monitoring and evaluation is required to know that how the adolescents are utilizing the information. Bring modifications accordingly.
- Media has a significant role to play. There is a need to have provision of telephonic counseling.
- There is a necessity to encourage students to ask questions. Put a box in the school in which students can drop their queries and addressed by the experts later.
- There is a need to work in coordination with parents, teachers and government/ policy makers. Like advertisements on HIV/AIDS, create awareness on reproductive health needs of adolescents.

Social Work Interventions

The above reflection on the findings, discussion and the recommendations offered by the adolescent students, teachers, and parents to impart reproductive health education to adolescents had set the background for developing the social work intervention model in order to design and strengthen the programme interventions for adolescents.

For designing any intervention model, the first and foremost issue to be considered is the target of intervention. The research being essentially on the adolescents, the adolescents, their teachers and parents will be considered the target of intervention in the model. The social worker would create a supportive and congenial environment for adolescents to gain knowledge on reproductive health issues. The social worker may liaison with the other professionals and agencies, acting as communicator and counselor and providing personal and emotional support. The endeavor should be on holistic intervention advocating for the involvement of people at different levels as given below in Figure 7.1: Social Work Intervention Model.

Target	Objectives	Activities
Adolescent students	• Creating Awareness on Reproductive health issues • Promoting Peer education • Forming Adolescents club	• Put a box in which students can drop their queries to be addressed by the experts • To collect Literature related to Reproductive health related issues (from the newspaper, magazines) and prepare magazine • Organizing competitions: Essay Writing/ Paragraph Writing, Slogan Writing, Debate , Painting (Poster, Rangoli): followed by group discussion and display (Bulletin Board and Wall Magazine display) • Quiz Contest • Puppet shows • Video shows • Brain storming exercises • Suggesting Internet Websites, books, novels, scientifically written on reproductive health issues. • Counseling sessions/telephonic
Parents	• Awareness building and sensitization Initiating Regular interaction between parents and teachers of adolescents • Initiating regular parent-child interaction	• Discussion on emerging issue of adolescents in every Parents Teacher Meeting (PTM) • Biannual-holding orientation workshop, seminars • Counseling sessions
Teachers	• Capacity building and sensitization • Initiating Regularinteraction between Parents and Teachers of adolescents • Making them accountable for their work	• Discussion on emerging issues of adolescents in every Parent Teacher Meeting (PTM) • Organizing training sessions, orientation workshop, seminars. • Counseling sessions
School Authorities: Principal, Management committee, and other staff members	• Sensitization on the need and importance of imparting reproductive health education to adolescents • Provision of adequate resource material, funds, other facilities to conduct RH education programme	• Meeting/Presentation with school administration about need objectives, work plan of reproductive health education. • Counseling session (if required)
Team of Professionals	• Networking/Strengthening linkages with other systems and enable concerted efforts for adolescents' development	• Holding regular meeting and interaction of the students, parents, and teachers with the professionals in the school. • Organize adolescents health camps • Develop print and visual material that offer accurate information on reproductive and sexual health issues to adolescents.
Policy Implementing Machinery	• Facilitate implementation of reproductive health education programmer at school system	• Facilitate in breaking barriers by talking on reproductive health education for adolescents. • Demand for a special department (consisted of social workers, and other professionals) in each school. • Demand to improve upon existing infrastructure.
Media	• Communicate rationale for addressing needs and concerns of adolescents on reproductive health issues	• Review of T.V. programmes, advertisements by especially constituted experts committee. • Establish linkages with media and organize talk shows where all the stakeholders (elected representative, teachers, parents, other professionals) can discuss face to face on adolescents needs and concerns.

Figure 7.1: Social Work Intervention Model

For imparting reproductive health education to adolescents in an effective way, the need is of working with various groups like, parents, teachers, principals, management committee of the schools, policy implementing machinery, team of professionals, and media. Interventions related to each target group are explained below:

Adolescent Students

The need to reach to adolescents with information and skills is of utmost importance. There is a necessity to create awareness on reproductive health issues amongst adolescents. Adolescents are particularly susceptible to peer pressure. Perceptions about what is accepted in their peer group and what their peers are doing have a considerable influence on their sexual behaviour. While peer pressure can lead them to an irresponsible behaviour, it can just as easily be a resource to be utilized for promoting desirable behaviour. The dissemination of information and behavioural change intervention may be routed though peer groups in a systematic manner in order to increase the pace and quantum of change. The findings on source of information also reflected that friends were considered to be the most reliable source of information. Hence, there is a need of promoting peer education, and forming adolescents club.

Parents

The parental acceptance and support is an important component of the success of programmes for adolescents is acknowledged because adolescents, especially girls, often need to be provided with adult permission and support to receive information on reproductive health issues. The findings of the present research suggest that the role of parents is critical in effective and sustainable change. Efforts are needed to develop this component and to make it an integrated part of the strategy. There is a need for awareness building and sensitization among parents on reproductive health issues, so that parents can adjust with changing times, remove generation gap, and increase communication with the adolescents. Schools need to give a platform for more parents' involvement so that the school together with parents can closely nurture the adolescents. Schools through the Parent-teacher-association can involve the parents for the developmental needs of the adolescent. If the school and parents work together many issues and problems of the adolescents can be tackled. Thus, there is a need to strengthen parents-teacher-association to initiate regular interaction between parents and teachers of adolescents and also initiating regular parent-child interaction.

Teachers

It has been noticed that the teachers are also not prepared and willing

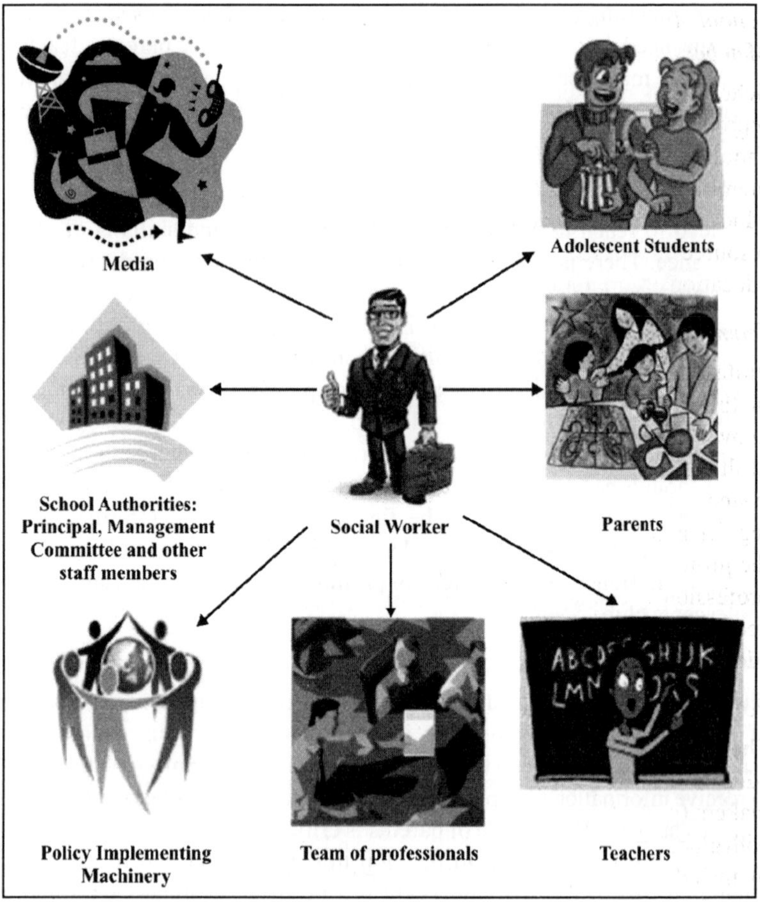

Figure 7.2: Pictorial Diagram

to discuss reproductive health issues with adolescents mostly because they feel uncomfortable while discussing such issues. Teachers, by and large, find the topic embarrassing and avoid it. Orientation and skill-building of teachers on adolescents' sexuality and reproductive health are urgently needed. Each subject teachers has a role in imparting reproductive health education. Therefore the urgent need is of capacity building and sensitization among teachers on reproductive health issues, initiating regular interaction between parents and teachers of adolescents, and making teachers accountable for their work. The social worker should invite experts to deal and work with the teachers and conduct workshops with them so that they feel comfortable in dealing with the issues of reproductive health with the adolescents.

School Authorities: Principal, Management Committee, and Other Staff Members

School authorities can help in enabling environment for implementation of reproductive health education in schools in a proper way. The social worker should sensitize the Principal, Management committee, and other staff members on the need and importance of imparting reproductive health education to adolescents. S/he should demand for provision of adequate resource materials, funds, other facilities to conduct reproductive health education programme.

Team of Professionals

Professionals in the area of reproductive health issues can bring about progress in the health status of the adolescents. They are considered the most knowledgeable persons and trusted source of information on reproductive health issues. The social worker should strengthen the linkages with other systems and enable concerted efforts for adolescents' development by holding regular meetings and interaction of the students, parents, and teachers with the professionals. The health camp can be conducted regularly. The help of professionals can be sought in developing print and visual material that offer accurate information on reproductive and sexual health issues to the adolescents.

Policy Implementing Machinery

The social worker should facilitate implementation of reproductive health education programme in the school system. They should sensitize decision makers (government officials) for pro adolescent approach keeping in tune with globalization, changing perceptions and expected demands as experienced by the adolescents. They should facilitate in breaking barriers by talking on reproductive health education for adolescents at public gatherings and meetings. Organize Conferences, seminars, and workshops; it would help in breaking barriers. demand for a special department (consisted of social workers, and other professional) in each school and also demand to improve upon existing infrastructure.

Media

Media should play a positive and constructive role by addressing the need of reproductive health education for adolescents. Media should help in breaking barriers on discussion of topic related to sexual and reproductive health. It should establish linkage with schools/ teachers and organize talk shows. Media should dedicate columns and programmes to address adolescents concerns. Media can provide a common platform for all stakeholders (elected representative, teachers, parents, and other professionals) to discuss adolescents' reproductive and sexual health needs. The review of T.V. programmes, advertisements can be done by the experts. In-depth case studies and features on issues for adolescents can be prepared and shown on T.V.

The social work intervention model as presented in Figure 7.1 will be utilized to impart reproductive health education to adolescents. The specific activities undertaken, with the various target groups are projected in the model. Figure 7.2 projected the pictorial diagram of the system where the social worker needs to intervene to facilitate smooth implementation of reproductive health education programme at school system.

Overall the book on reproductive health education to adolescents had been a worthwhile attempt. This book scientifically presented the detailed account of the level of knowledge and perception of the adolescents regarding reproductive health issues, and various source of information accessed by them for gaining the knowledge on reproductive health issues. Adolescents as well their parents and teachers recognized the need and importance of imparting reproductive health education at school system. However, being a sensitive issue, talking on reproductive health issues would require adequate knowledge and information in conjunction with the social norms of society. It would also necessitate specialized helping service and time and the Social Work being a helping profession would continue to play a significant role in rendering the appropriate services for the smooth and speedy implementation of reproductive health education to adolescents at school level.

References

Abraham, L. (1998). *Understanding youth sexuality: A study of college students in Mumbai, India.* Mumbai: Tata Institute of Social Sciences.

Abraham, L. (2001). Understanding youth sexuality: A study of college students in Mumbai city. *The Indian Journal of Social Work,* 62, 233-248.

Abraham, L., and Kumar, K.A. (1999). Sexual experiences and their correlates among college students in Mumbai city, India. *International Family Planning Perspectives,* 25, 139-146.

Acharya, S.S., and R. Dasgupta. (2005). HIV/ AIDS and adolescents: Some issues and concerns from India. *Indian Journal of Social Work,* 35(1-2), 123-137.

Adler, A. (1964). *The Individual Psychology of Alfred Adler.* New York: Harper Torchbooks.

Aggarwal, A., and Kumar, R. (1997). Awareness of AIDS among school children in Haryana. Indian Journal of Public Health, 40, 38-45.

Ahuja, A., and Tewari, S. (1995). Awareness of pubertal changes among adolescent girls. *The Journal of Family Welfare,* 41 (1), 46-50.

Amalraj, E.R. *et al.,* (1997). First Year Medical Students' AIDS knowledge and attitude. In O.P. Aggarwal, A.K. Sharma, and A. Indrayan (eds.), *HIV/ AIDS Research in India* (pp. 243-246). New Delhi: NACO, Ministry of Health and Family Welfare, GOI.

Arber, S. (2001). Secondary analysis of survey data. In N. Gilbert (Ed.), *Researching Social Life.* (pp. 58-84). London: Sage Publications.

Atwood, S.J., and Hussein, J. (1997). Adolescent motherhood: Priorities and next steps. *The Journal of Family Welfare,* 43 (2), 8-14.

Awasthi, S., and Pande, V.K. (1998). Sexual behaviour patterns and knowledge of sexually transmitted diseases in adolescent boys in urban slums of Lucknow, north India. *Indian Pediatrics,* 35, 1105-1109.

Bahulekar, P.V., and Garg, B.S. (1997). AIDS awareness in school children. In O.P. Aggarwal, A.K. Sharma, and A. Indrayan (Eds.), *HIV/AIDS Research in India* (pp. 181-188). New Delhi: NACO, Ministry of Health and Family Welfare, GOI.

Bancroft, J., and Reinisch, J.M. (1990). *Adolescence and Puberty.* Oxford University Press.

Bandura, A. (1969). Social-learning Theory of Identificatory Processes. In D.A. Goslin (Ed.), *Handbook of Socialization: Theory and Research.* Chicago: Rand McNally.

Bandura, A. (1973). *Agression: A Social Learning Analysis*. New Jersey: Englewood Cliffs. Prentice-Hall.

Basanayake, S. (1985). Knowledge and Attitude about Reproductive Health among Young in Srilanka. *Journal of Family Welfare*, 33 (4).

Berger, D. (2005). Sex *education: teachers' and future teachers' Conceptions and social representations; what Relevance for teachers' training?* IOSTE symposium, the use of science and technology education for peace and sustainable development.

Bhasin, S.K. *et al.*, (1997). Knowledge and attitudes amongst school children regarding AIDS in East Delhi. In O.P. Aggarwal, A.K. Sharma,. and A. Indrayan (eds.), *HIV/ AIDS Research in India* (pp. 166-170). New Delhi: NACO, Ministry of Health and Family Welfare, GOI.

Bhasin, S.K., and Aggarwal, O.P. (1999). Perceptions of teachers regarding Sex education in National Capital Territory of Delhi. *Indian Journal of Pediatrics,* 66(4), 527-531.

Bhatia, V., and H. M. Swami. (2000). Fertility Control methods: Knowledge of adolescent girls in school of Chandigarh. *Indian Journal of Medical Sciences,* 54(8), 342-346.

Bhende, A. (1995). A study of sexuality of adolescent girls and Boys in underprivileged groups in Bombay. *The Indian Journal of Social Work,* 55(4), 557- 571.

Black, J., and Champion, D.J. (1976). *Methods and Issues in Social Research.* New York: John Wiley and Sons.

C.B.S.E. (2009). Annual Report 2009. New Delhi: Central Board of Secondary Examination.

Census of India. (2001). *Census of India.* [Electronic Version]. Retrieved on 2nd January, 2008. From http://censusindia.gov.in/Data_Products/Library/Provisional_Population_Total_link/webed.html

Center for Operations Research and Training (CORT). (1999). *Health of pregnant women and adolescents in India. Review of literature: A summary report.* Baroda: CORT.

Chakrabarti, (2003). Population education in formal and non-formal sectors in India. In S. Bott *et al.*, (Eds.), *Towards Adulthood: Exploring the Sexual and Reproductive Health of Adolescents inSouth Asia*. (pp. 165-167). Geneva: World Health Organisation.

Chaudhary, R.H. (1998). *Socio-economic, demographic and reproductive health profiles of adolescents in SAARC countries.* Paper presented at the South Asia Conference on Adolescents, New Delhi.

Clarke, A. (2001). Research and the policy-making process. In N. Gilbert (Ed.), *Researching Social Life.* (pp. 28-44). London: Sage Publications.

Coleman, J. J. (1978). Current Contradictions in Adolescent Theory. *Journal of Youth and Adolescence*. 7, 1-11.

Dash, R. (2004).Reproductive health Problems of Unmarried Adolescent Girls. In Tata Institute of Social Sciences (TISS) (Ed.) *Adolescent Health and Related Issues:* Vol. II. Mumbai: TISS.

Directorate of Education. (2009 a). *Yuva school life skills Programme.* [Electronic Version]. Retrieved on March 12, 2010 from, Delhi: Directorate of Education.

Directorate of Education. (2009 b). *Yuva helpline.* [Electronic Version]. Retrieved on March 12, 2010 from, Delhi: Directorate of Education.

Emerson, R.; Fretz, R.; and Shaw, L. (1995). *Writing Ethnographic Fieldnotes.* Chiicago: University of Chicago Press.

Erikson, E.H. (1968). *Identity, Youth and Crisis.* London: Faber and Faber.

Focus Adolescent Services (n.d.). *The major task of adolescence.* Retrieved on 12th December 2009.

Freud, A. (1948). *The Ego and the Mechanisms of Defense.* New York: International Universities Press.

Gall, M.D.; Borg, W.R., and Gall, J.P. (1996). *Education research: An introduction* (6th ed.). NY: Longman: White Plains.

Ganatra, B. (2000). Abortion Research in India: What we now. In R. Ramasubban, and S. Jejeebhoy (Eds.), *Women's Reproductuve Health in India.* (pp.186-235). New Delhi: Rawat Publication.

Ganatra, B., and Hirve, S. (2002). Induced abortions among adolescent women in rural Maharashtra. *Reproductive Health Matters*, 10, 76-85.

Gardner, L. and Elliot, A. (1975). *Handbook of social psychology.* New Delhi: Amerind Publishing Co.

George, J. (2004). Knowledge and Attitude Related to Reproductive Health of Adolescents. In Tata Institute of Social Sciences (TISS) (Ed.) *Adolescent Health and Related Issues*: Vol. III. Mumbai: TISS.

Government of India. (1998). *National Policy on Education (as modified in 1992).* New Delhi: Department of Education, Ministry of Human Resource Development, Government of India.

Government of India. (2000). *National Population Policy of India.* New Delhi: Ministry of Health and Family Welfare, Government of India.

Government of India. (2001). *The National Policy for the Empowerment of Women.* Department of Women and Child Development. New Delhi: Ministry of Human Resource Development, Government of India.

Government of India. (2002). *National Health Policy.* New Delhi: Ministry of Health and Family Welfare, Government of India.

Government of India. (2003). *National Youth Policy-2003.* New Delhi: Ministry of Youth Affairs and Sports, Government of India.

Government of India. (2006). *Reproductive and child health programme.* New Delhi: Department of Family Welfare, Ministry of Health and Family Welfare, Government of India.

Grouter, A.C., and Booth, A. (2003). *Just Living Together: Implications of Cohabitation on Families, Children, and Social Policy.* Penn State University Family Issues Symposia Series: Routledge Publications.

Gupta, A.; Mehta, S.; Ghate, M.; Reynolds, S.; Sahay, S., and Godbole, S. (2004). *Same—sex behaviour, sexually transmitted infections (STI) and HIV risks among men attending STI clinics in Pune, India.* 1993-2002. XV International AIDS Conference; Bangkok, Thailand.

Gupta, R.B., and Khan, M.E. (1996). Teenage fertility: Some results from a baseline survey in Uttar Pradesh. *The Journal of Family Welfare,* 42 (2), 14-20.

Hall, G.S. (1904). *Adolescence: Its Psychology and Its Relation to Physiology, Anthropology, Sociology, Sex, Crime, Religion and Education.* New York: D. Appleton and Co.

Harms, G.; Corea, A.; Iyambo, S.; Radebe, F.; Fehler, H., and Ballard, R. (1998). *Perceptions and patterns of reproductive tract infections in a young rural population in Namibia.* In 2nd European Congress on Tropical Medicine. UK: Liverpool.

Hart, C. (1998). *Doing a literature review: Releasing the social science research imagination.* London: Sage.

Havighurst, R.J. (1951). *Developmental Tasks and Education.* New York: Longmans, Green.

Hurlock, E.B. (1967). *Adolescent Development.* New York: McGraw- Hill Book Company.

Ingersoll, G. (n.d.). *Developmental Tasks of Normal Adolescence.* Center for Studies. Indiana, USA. [Electronic Version]. Retrieved on 24 June 2008.

International Institute for Sustainable Development (IISD). (1999). Summary of the 21st special session of the General Assembly (ICPD=5). *Earth Negotiation Bulletin.* 6(61), 1-13.

Jejeebhoy, S. (1995). *Women's Education Autonorny And Reproductive Behaviour Experiences From Developing Contries.* Oxford: Oxford University Press.

Jejeebhoy, S. (1996). *Adolescent sexual and reproductive behaviour: A review of evidence from India.* ICRW Working Paper no. 3. Washington, DC: International Centre for Research on Women.

Jejeebhoy, S.J. (2000). Adolescent sexual and reproductive behaviour: A review of the evidence from India. In R. Ramasubban and S.J. Jejeebhoy (Eds.), *Women's reproductive health in India,* (pp. 40-101). Jaipur: Rawat Publications.

Kamat, T.V. (1996). Teenage pregnancy: Some associated risk factors—A review. In S. Rao, and A. Kanade, (Eds.), *Proceedings of National Workshop on Adolescence: Need for Critical Appraisal,* (pp. 66-73). Pune, Maharashtra, India: Department of Biometry and Nutrition, Agharkar Research Institute.

Kelefang, B., and Lennéer, B.A. (2008). *Sexuality Education in Sweden: A study based on research and young people's service providers in Gothenburg.* [Electronic Version]. Retrieved on 3rd, January, 2009.

Kenneth, B. (1982). *Methods of Social Research.* New York: The Free Press.

Khan, I.; Lakhanpal, S.; Khan, W.; Sinha, R., and Vishwakarma, J. (1996). *Knowledge, attitude and sexual behaviour of school going adolescents in Uttar Pradesh.* Paper presented at the workshop on Youth and Population, jointly organized by the Center for Operations Research and Training and the Rajiv Gandhi National Institute of Youth Development: Baroda, Gujarat.

Khan, M.A., and Singh, P. (1997). A study to evaluate the impact of AIDS education among college and university students at Agra. In O.P. Aggarwal, A.K. Sharma, and A. Indrayan (Eds.). *HIV/AIDS Research in India,* (pp. 760-766). New Delhi: NACO, Ministry of Health and Family Welfare, GOI.

Khisbiyah; Yayah; Desti, M., and Wijayanto. (1997). *Unwanted Pregnancy among Adolescents.* New York: Population Research Center, University of Gadjah Mada.

Kirby, D. (2001). Understanding what works and what doesn't in reducing adolescent sexual risk-taking. *Family Planning Perspectives*, 33(6), 276-281.

Lal, P., Kumar; A., Ingle; G.K., and Gulati, N. (1997). Knowledge and attitudes of university students regarding HIV/AIDS: An urban-rural difference. In O.P.

Aggarwal, A.K. Sharma, and A. Indrayan (Eds.), HIV/AIDS Research in India (pp. 224-227). New Delhi: NACO, Ministry of Health and Family Welfare, GOI.

Lal Das, D.K. (2000). *Practice of Social Research: Social Work Perspective.* Jaipur: Rawat Publications.

LeCompte, M.D.; Klinger, J.K.; Campbell S.A., and Menke, D.W. (2003). Editor's introduction. *Review of Educational Research,* 73(2), 123-124.

MAMTA Health Institute for Mother and Child. (2001). *Adolescent Health and Development in India: An Action Approach.* New Delhi: MAMTA.

Manju, (2006). *Utilization of reproductive health services by the women in an urban slum of Delhi.* M.Phil., Unpublished work. Delhi.

Masilamani, R. (2003). Building a supportive environment for adolescent reproductive health programmes: Essential programme components. In S. Bott and S.J. Jeejebhoy (Eds.), *Towards adulthood: Exploring the sexual and reproductive health of adolescents in South Asia,* (pp. 156-158). Geneva: World Health Organization.

Maslow, A.H. (1943). A Theory of Human Motivation. *Psychological Review,* 50, 370-96.

McCabe, M.P. (1996). Sex education programmes for people with mental retardation. *Mental Retardation,* 31, 377-387.

McManus, A., and Dhar, L. (2008). *Study of knowledge, perception and attitude of adolescent girls towards STIs/HIV, safer sex and sex education: (A cross sectional survey of urban adolescent school girls in South Delhi, India)* [Electronic version]. Retrieved on April 12, 2009 from http://www.biomedcentral.com/1472-6874/8/12

Mead, M. (1950). *Coming of Age in Samoa.* New York: New American Library.

Mead, M. (1953). *Growing up in New Guinea.* New York: Mentor Books.

Mehra, S.; Savithri, R., and Coutinho, L. (2002). *Sexual behaviour among adolescents and young people in India: Some emerging trends.* (Working paper series 3). New Delhi: MAMTA.

Monette, D.R.; Sullivian, T.J.; and Dejong, C.R. (2002). *Applied Social research: Tools for the human services.* United States of America: Thomson learning Academic Resource Centre.

NACO, MOHFW, and GOI (2005): *UNGASS (United Nations General Assembley Special Session On HIV/AIDS) India Report: Progress Report on the Declaration of Commitment on HIV/AIDS.* New Delhi: National AIDS Control Organization, Ministry of Health and Family Welfare, Government of India.

National AIDS Control Organisation (NACO) and UNICEF. (2002). *Knowledge, attitudes and practices of young adults (15-24 years).* New Delhi: NACO and UNICEF.

National AIDS Control Organisation (NACO). (2002). *National AIDS Prevention and Control Policy.* New Delhi: NACO.

National Council of Educational Research and Training (NCERT). (2000). *National Curriculum Framework for School Education.* New Delhi: NCERT.

Onifade, I. (1999). *Unmet Reproductive Needs of Adolescents: Implications of HIV/AIDS Prevention in Africa.* Canberra: National Centre for Epidemiological and Population Health and Australian National University.

Patel, and Andrew. (2001). Gender, sexual abuse and risk behaviours in adolescents: A crosssectional survey in schools in Goa. *National Medical Journal of India,* 14(5), 263-67.

Pati, R.N. (2004). *Adolescent Girls.* Delhi: A.P.H. Publishing Corporation.

Patterson, G.R., and Fisher, P.A. (2002). Recent developments in our understanding of parenting: Bidirectional effects, causal models, and the search for parsimony. In M. Bornstein (Ed.), *Handbook of parenting: Practical and applied parenting,* pp. 59-88.

Piaget, J. (1952). *The Origins of Intelligence in Children.* New York: International Press.

Planning Commission, (2001). *Report of the Working Group on Adolescents for the Tenth Five Year Plan.* GOI, Planning Commission.

Planning Commission. (2002). *Tenth Five Year Plan (2002-2007).* Vol. 2. New Delhi: Planning Commission, Government of India.

Planning Commission. (2006). *Report of the working group on adolescents for Eleventh Five-Year plan.* New Delhi: Planning Commission, Government of India.

Population Council. (1999). *Adolescents in Transition: Programme and Practices in India.* Population Council.

Prasad, M.B. (2006). Perception on Sexual Matters Among Rural Adolescent Boys: A study in Andhra Pradesh. In C.P. Prakasam and S. Siva Raju (Eds.), *Adolescents Reproductive Health Perspectives.* (pp. 73-88). Delhi: B.R. Publishing Corporation.

Pratinidhi, A. (1996). Adolescent pregnancies (Plenary Lecture V). In S. Rao and A. Kanade (Eds.), *Proceedings of National Workshop on Adolescence: Need for Critical Appraisal,* (pp.129-137). Pune, Maharashtra, India: Department of Biometry and Nutrition, Agharkar Research Institute.

Rahate, N.P.; Zodpey, S.P.; and Bhalkule, P.R. (1997). AIDS awareness amongst rural junior college students. In O.P. Aggarwal, A.K. Sharma, and A. Indrayan (Eds.), *HIV/AIDS Research in India,* (pp. 222-223). New Delhi: NACO, Ministry of Health and Family Welfare, Government of India.

Rao, (1995). The Need and Challenge of Adolescent Health. *Health for the Millions, May-June.*

Rajiv Gandhi National Institute for Youth Development (RGNIYD). (2007 a). *Youth in India Report.* [Electronic Version] Retrieved on 12th April, 2008.

Rajiv Gandhi National Institute for Youth Development (RGNIYD). (2007 b). *Youth in India Report.* [Electronic Version] Retrieved on 12th April, 2008.

Sachdev, P. (1998). Sex on campus: A preliminary study of knowledge, attitudes and behaviour of university students in Delhi, India. *Journal of Biosocial Science,* 30, 95-105.

Sahoo, P.K. (2004). Level of Knowledge on Sexual Health Education among Unmarried adolescents. In Tata Institute of Social Sciences (TISS) (Ed.) *Adolescent Health and Related Issues:* Vol. III. Mumbai: TISS.

Santrock, J.W. (2004). *Child development* (10th ed.). New York: McGraw-Hill.

Selman, R.L. (1980). *The growth of interpersonal understanding.* New York: Academic Press.

Sharma, A., and Sharma, V. (1996). Sexual knowledge and practices of college girls in rural Gujarat, India. *The Journal of Family Welfare,* 42 (3), 19-26.

Sharma, V., and Sharma, A. (1995). The letter-box approach—A model for sex education in an orthodox society. *The Journal of Family Welfare,* 41 (4), 31-34.

Sharma, V., and Sharma, A. (1997). Adolescent boys in Gujarat, India: Their sexual behaviour and their knowledge of acquired immunodeficiency syndrome and other sexually transmitted diseases. *The Journal of Developmental and Behavioural Pediatrics,* 18 (6), 399-404.

Shilpa, V., and Ratnakumari, S. (1999). Knowledge of high school students on reproductive health and AIDS. *Indian Psychological Review,* 52 (1), 14-23.

Simmons, R. (2001). Questionnaires. In N. Gilbert (Ed.), *Researching Social Life.* London: Sage Publications.

Singh, M.M.; R. Devi, and S.S. Gupta, (1999). Awareness and health seeking behaviour of rural adolescent school girls on menstrual and reproductive health problems. *Indian Journal of Medical Sciences,* 53(9), 439-43.

Sundar, M.; Kavitha, J.; Mathai, L.M., and Manjunath, C. (1997). Knowledge of AIDS among student population in Bangalore city. In O.P. Aggarwal, A.K. Sharma, and A. Indrayan (Eds.), *HIV/AIDS Research in India,* pp. 236-240. New Delhi: NACO, Ministry of Health and Family Welfare, Government of India.

Swamy, S.S., (2005). *Population and development education.* volume-II. Hyderabad: Neelkamal Publications.

Thakor, H.G., and Kumar, P. (2000). Impact assessment of school-based sex education programme amongst adolescents. *Indian Journal of Pediatrics,* 67 (8), 551-558.

Thapa, V.J., and Rawal, S. (1998). An early awakening. *India Today,* 52-56.

Tikoo, M.; Bollman, S.R., and Bergen, M.B. (1997). Knowledge level of youth in India regarding human sexuality and AIDS. In O.P. Aggarwal, A.K. Sharma and A. Indrayan (Eds.), *HIV/AIDS Research in India,* (pp. 208-215). New Delhi: NACO, Ministry of Health and Family Welfare, Government of India.

Umamani, K.S., and Raju, K.N.M. (1997). Cultural factors and prepuberty marriages in Karnataka. *Man in India,* 77 (4), 363-374.

UN Millennium Project, (2005). *UN Millennium Project. Investing in development: a practical plan to achieve the Millennium Development Goals.* New York: UN.

United Nations Population Fund (UNFPA) (1998). *Socioeconomic demographic and reproductive health profiles of adolescents in SAARC countries.* South-Asia Conference on the adolescents, 21-23 July 1998. New Delhi: India.

UNFPA. (2003). *The State of World Population.* Retrieved on 4th November, 2008.

United Nation (UN), (1994). *Summary of the programme of action of the International Conference on Population and Development (ICPD).* Cairo: UN.

United Nation Population Fund. (2005) *Adolescents in India: A Profile.* Retrieved on 12th July, 2010.

Uplaonkar, A.T. (1995). The emerging rural youth: A study of their changing values towards marriage. *The Indian Journal of Social Work, LW* (4), 415-423.

US Census Bureau. (2005): *U.S. Census Bureau, International Database.* April 2005. IDB Summary Demographic Data for India. Retrieved on 14th October, 2008.

Verma, S., and Pauri, K.M. (1997). A rapid survey to assess AIDS awareness among college students in Bombay and Pune. In O.P. Aggarwal, A.K. Sharma, and A. Indrayan (Eds.), *HIV/AIDS Research in India,* pp. 228-233. New Delhi: NACO, Ministry of Health and Family Welfare, Government of India.

World Health Organisation (WHO). (1986). *Young People's health: A challenge for society.* Geneva: WHO series 73.

World Health Organisation (WHO). (1996). *Identifying Needs and Developing a National Strategy for Reproductive Health.* Geneva: WHO.

World Health Organisation (WHO). (1999). *Programming for Adolescent Health and Development*. Report of a WHO/UNFPA/UNICEF study group on programming for adolescent health (World Health Organisation Technical Report Series No. 886: i-vi, 1-260). Geneva: WHO.

World Health Organisation (WHO). (2006). *A Reference Guide to Policies and Practices; Sexuality Education.* Geneva: WHO.

Yadav, S. (2003). A study of Awareness and Attitude of Students towards Adolescent Reproductive Health. *Indian Educational Review,* 39(1), New Delhi: NCERT.